BROKEN

BROKEN

A Never-Ending Journey

by

Louise Bourdon

Copyright 2024 Louise Bourdon

TRIGGER WARNING

To whoever may read this- I would just like to let you know firstly my reason for informing you of this page 'Trigger Warning.' It is to safeguard anyone that may have experienced a traumatic event in their lifetime or even still going through.

My book contains a lot of mention of rape, torture, and abuse. Grief, mental and physical health, and suicide I have been through and still living with.

I understand that it is not okay for me to just assume you will be all right with everything I have written however, I have made it clear on each poem and letter with a 'TRIGGER WARNING' that I believe can be distressing and that may upset someone.

If at any point, the content in my book may be triggering or disturbing for you in any way, then please skip those poems and letters.

Take care of yourself.

I am falling.

Only, there is no one to catch me.

As each day comes to an end,

I drown in the darkness

that closes in around me,

buried within my troubles.

I may as well be invisible,

for no one sees my pain, my tears,

or hear my screams

that pierce the stillness in the night.

I was once whole,

but for so long now

I have had to live… not as one,

but as a thousand, tiny pieces-

A kaleidoscope rotating-

Not of colour…only black remains

trapped in a prism, most fail to see.

My shards splintered, my loose fragments,

the individual elements of my life

that no one can fix,

for only I am aware of every jagged edge

that cuts deep into my fragile skin.

For only I understand the deepness

of what eats away at me….

Only I can see the endless darkness

of fear that blinds 'my world,'

and there is nothing I can do….

For my soul is

'Broken.'

CONTENTS

PREFACE

This book has a mixture of both poems and letters. From physical health disorders, to mental health disorders, including PTSD, intrusive nightmares and trauma. From reflecting to being lost and alone to living in a dark world, trying to survive, convincing myself that I am broken and generally troubled. From my stroke to loneliness. Grief, heartbreak, and memories. From desperation, anxiety, depression, fear, rape, to suicide, to goodbyes, to heaven. Each page in this book contains nothing but my own experiences of how my life has been and continues to be. I know that I can never fix myself, that is down to the help of the professionals. I am just here to share with you how my life has been and how I am trying so hard to keep moving forward. This is about my journey of over 36 years, reflecting on my lifelong battles. Some of the darkest times I have had and still have. Some bad enough to scar me for life. I have written this book because I do not want to hide away anymore and I want to let you all know that neither do you have to. It is based upon my life experiences in which some are very deep and upsetting, so I apologize for that. In every single page that you read, I have been both honest and open. However, you will notice that in some of my poems and letters I mention the word 'Demon.' This is because I cannot name the man that raped me for legal reasons. However, I will not be silent anymore about what he did and how he has destroyed my life….

This book has been a very long time coming and has taken me a considerable amount of time to prepare, making sure I was to get every word in it right. I had written most of the book by October 2022 but unfortunately had to have a long break from it due to my stroke in the November and recovery and my dad sadly passing away in January 2023. I am glad that I can finally share it with all of you, and I am sure there are many of you that will read this, that will really get it and understand it, but I also get that there may be many people that just do not, but that is okay. Not everyone is going to feel the same or agree for that matter. I am not even sure if all this collection is for everyone as a lot of them mention some very deep and traumatic things, although you can skip those pages if you wish to.

I am not a professional so unable to give any advice. But if you are experiencing anything that you read that sounds like you, please seek the correct help. There are many numbers at the end of the book for you to be able to contact.

THIS IS ME

(Trigger Warning: This contains mention of rape, death, suicide, mental and physical health)

There has been a lot that has happened in my life and I know there are far worse off people than me. There will always be far worse off people than me, but I have chosen to write this book because I don't want to hide anymore. I don't want to stay trapped in this life of mine. This is not just about what has happened in my lifetime as in losing my loved ones. This is also about what happened to me that no one, not even my family know about. It is not every day you tell the world about yourself, especially when a lot of the things have been a secret for over three decades. I have spent most of my life fighting a silent battle. It has never been about not being able to be open with what has happened or how I am feeling because I have been brought up to be able to reach out and talk to my parents, talk to anyone about anything and normally I would, but I found I was not able to do it. So, here I am, about to tell the world, how my life has been…

Just over 36 years ago, I was brutally raped. By brutal I mean violently, viciously beaten, and raped. It has physically, emotionally, and psychologically crushed me and I am still living with this now. He violated me and stripped away my dignity and I re live what he did, every single day and night. This trauma has haunted me ever since, and I do not just mean the physical effects that it has on me, but the mental effects to. The flashbacks, nightmares, intrusive thoughts.

3

Severe anxiety and depression. The suicidal thoughts. Not being able to trust people. Looking over my shoulder in fear. The person I confided in about what happened to me, made me feel as though I was the criminal, so I never took it any further and never told anyone else about what happened that night, just kept it to myself. The rape has since left me too scared to be alone with anyone or trust anyone and I have developed a negative outlook on life because I feel damaged. My whole world was turned upside down that night and it has left me feeling totally scared ever since. I still feel sick, dirty, and numb. I have been left feeling helpless and alone and I do not think I will ever get over what happened to me. It is not something that can just be 'fixed' or that I am suddenly going to feel 'safe.' Several months after I was brutally raped, I discovered I was pregnant. I could not believe how it was even possible, as I was on the pill! The result was not what I expected after the horrifying ordeal that 'demon' put me through. There was no way I could keep the baby as too many damaging memories, as you can imagine, so I had him adopted. One of the hardest decisions I ever had to make. Neither was I prepared for all the questions as to where the baby had suddenly gone! I never even saw him. It was not his fault, I know that. But how could I keep him? Forever being reminded of what happened to me that night.

Looking at it now, what I went through that night, I believe is what pushed me completely over the edge. I could have ended my life, here I am still living to tell you all what happened. I could have died. But I have continued to live on, to share my story.

Over the years, many other upsetting things have happened, including the sad loss of my grandson, step sister, step dad and my partner's mum. I suffered a miscarriage; it made me feel as though it was my punishment for giving up the baby that the 'demon' had forcibly put inside me. Yet I have had to live with this for years, with no one knowing. Both my mental health and physical health seemed to suffer more and more as the years went on. I was eventually diagnosed with musculoskeletal disorders (osteoarthritis and prolapsed discs in my spine and neck and then I had a bad accident and seriously damaged both my shoulders. I had to have 14 operations in total and they are still not right now which is why I suffer with Tendonitis. I also have glaucoma and had to have operation done on both my eyes. I have felt as though I have been taking more and more and it has led me to believe this is how my life is supposed to be. If it is not something bad that has happened to me or still happening, then it is the sad, ongoing tragedies that have happened to others that are sadly affecting me. I have felt myself sinking lower and lower and I have struggled to find a way forward, pretending to be alright but really, I am falling apart. People think I am okay, but the truth is, I am not. In fact, it all got so bad trying to cope with everything and hiding my secret also for so long, it finally took its toll on me and I attempted to take my own life. I never told a sole, I never planned it, I just did it and at the time I did not want to be found. I just wanted to be free from the pain I was feeling, both physically and mentally. I never believed I could ever do it, but having the intense feelings of not being able to cope any longer and faced with overwhelming thoughts, I honestly felt it was the only way in which I could stop hurting.

I did not plan it, but it was after this that I finally got diagnosed with mental health disorders, ptsd, depression, and anxiety/panic attacks. Sadness did not stop though, because in April 2020, my partner passed away suddenly from a stroke and sepsis. My heart was broken and my world fell apart. I could not believe he was gone. I sunk lower and lower and it felt like my life had just got a whole lot worse. I have never talked to anyone about it because I have believed that no one would understand how I am feeling. This has all taken a huge knock on my mental health, adding to everything else I have been trying so hard to cope with and sadly, it led me to yet more attempts to end my life. No one knows when I have done this or how many times. It has not been the sort of thing I have wanted to broadcast because people do not get it. No one that hasn't ever felt suicidal could ever possibly understand how I feel. My mental health has deteriorated even more since and I have been trying to cope with everything, as well as my love no longer being here. I have not wanted to live my life anymore. I have not wanted to live at all because I have not been able to cope with all that has been going on in my head, I have just wanted it to stop.

In November 2022 I had another knock back. I had a stroke. Out of nowhere I suddenly lost my sight. My peripheral vision (which is my side vision) went completely in both eyes. I have 80% of it now. The best I am ever going to get. I lost control of my left side and my short-term memory was and still is, non-existent which causes me great difficulty finding the right words and understanding a lot of what others are saying, plus I am so forgetful. That is because that part of my brain is dead and it will not ever come back. My depression and anxiety are more through the roof than they have ever been and I am snappy most of the time which gets me frustrated! As you can imagine, this has all been so scary. I never believed I would survive.

 In January 2023 my dad suddenly passed away. I had only spoken to him a couple of days before, it never made sense. It was yet another huge knock to my very fragile self, so as you can probably imagine, I am feeling pretty rubbish. I waited for what seemed like forever, before finally being allocated a mental health care co- ordinator. But she had to leave, and I was back on the waiting list. My next mental health worker also left, so once again I had to cope alone. Eventually, I was allocated someone new and a peer support worker and began getting the professional help that I needed. I have a long way to go, but somehow, I am continuing with my life. Smile and just pretend that I am fine, even though deep down I know I am not. I guess it is all I can do!

INTRODUCTION

If you are reading this right now, then I wish to thank you with all my heart. I am truly grateful that you are taking a precious moment of your time to read through this. I am here to share with you some of the toughest times in my life. Times that I never thought I would ever get through. My book is a range of poems and short letters from life, to struggles, to loss. It is dark and unsettling in places as it conveys the thoughts and feelings of my life. The effects it has and the impact on my day- to -day life, making things that others might not think about, a bit more difficult. Highlighting the hardships of living with heartbreak, to grieving, to the everyday flashbacks that have haunted me for over 36 years and still do. To the daily battles of my mental health disorders that I have carried with me for many years to my physical health disorders, which have led to ongoing operations. To the sad and distressing times of my suicide attempts when things have become almost impossible for me to carry on and with each poem and letter that you read, it will allow you to understand how my life has been for me and still is, but also how life may be for you too and I want you to know that you are not alone in your thoughts or challenges. I have wanted to write this book for so long but was never quite sure if it was the right thing to do. I just knew I had to get my feelings and thoughts out there. It has only taken me 36 years to be open and I know I still have a long way to go, no matter how many times I have given up. There is so much more to a lot of lives than most people even realize and in reading this book you will understand where I am coming from.

It has made me be open about my every-day life and it documents the serious reality of living the way I have for such a long time. It gives an in- depth detail of my day- to- day struggles and in reading this it will make you realize what I am all about. Maybe, this book will make you think! Think about how some of these things could be familiar to your own life, or someone you know. I understand everyone has a life of challenges. Whether it be some form of trauma or loss even every day stresses of life, physically or mentally. It can all become overwhelming.

For me, writing my poems and letters have helped me through so many of my dark times. As much as some of the ones I have written are very deep, it is all about helping me process and I hope if any that you read also relate to you or your life, that you to may just be able to understand that you do not have to hide. I have not written this book for sympathy. I have not written it to just be able to tell you how my life is through the trauma I have suffered, the loss I have been dealt, the hope that I have prayed for and the tears that I have cried. I have written this because I want to be honest. To open- up. To stop hiding and because this has been my life for the last 36 years.

There may well be a lot of you that will possibly think my writing is too dark and that some of them are very deep and may trigger off certain things. I am trying to get my thoughts and feelings out there and as the reader, I want you to know that you do not have to hide from your disorders, or your worries and fears, or sadness.

I know only too well what it is like to put on that fake smile. I know I am not a professional and neither do I have any answers. But all I can do, is tell you how it is for me and the help I am getting, the people that are helping me, are the people that can help you to. It is a journey that is never ending' and there will always be battles which will test us along the way, but in time with professional help, all we can hope for is that we can all slowly move forward.

I am sharing my life for those that don't have a voice! For those that are too scared to speak up. This was me once. But here I am now…. Telling my story. Telling the truth.

Thank you for reading.

Louise x

REFLECTION

Who is this woman?

With the ashen look and fragile lines

that are drawn into each sunken cheek.

A shattered heart and soul that is weary,

tired eyes from empty promises of sleep.

Her hair limp and lifeless,

skin faded into a grey dismay.

Deep lines around her eyes,

her face a touch of grey.

She is like the rain in the storm,

the snow in the winter,

the seed waiting to grow.

Spiralled into a world of hurt

that no one will ever know.

Embracing the silent stirrings in her soul

reflecting on the layers only she can see.

She looks again… As she whispers to herself

The 'reflection' in the mirror…is ME

MY REFLECTION

The 'reflection' is me…. It is who I see each morning when I look in the mirror. I see this tired, sad, depressed, destroyed, tear-stained, broken person that has lost my looks, my smile, my get up and go …from a broken heart of tragedy and let downs, trauma and abuse, illnesses, and loneliness. It is so hard when I cannot love myself for who I am, no matter how hard I try. That constant fear of having to face seeing myself in the mirror and the person I see looking back at me is not what I want to see, and then I start hearing these voices in my head telling me that I do not look good. When I look at myself, I just see this broken woman with eyes full of sadness. I get that I carry these deep lines in my face and that my hair is greying, but I don't like the person that I am. I don't like what I see in the mirror. The visual perception of myself is a broken-down figure in black and white. Empty and cold. Just an ugly, destroyed, and tired mess that has totally lost myself. I hate the person I see, staring back at me, looking sad and distressed. I am unable to recognize any strengths, only my weaknesses. This highly critical woman, who holds so many negative emotions.

All I can ever see in the mirror is a distortion of myself, a reflection of my flaws. It shows me my true feelings and that I do not belong in this life and no matter what mirror I look in, they all show me that there are no positives and that I will forever be stuck with this image. I cannot be perfect, I know that. Neither can I always be a picture of perfection. But I do wish that I could see a better me. Just once!

Or will it always be, that I look in the mirror and all I see are the fractured pieces in my crumbling skin as I cry several tears onto the breaking glass in front of me…

I guess it is called Life!

AM I LOST?

I keep asking myself

am I lost?

In this place called life!

I keep on going down that same road.

The one that leads to nowhere…

A path of confusion-

A dead end.

In the darkest of moments

surrounded by silence,

I delve into the rivers of my thoughts,

tangled up within my emotions

as teardrops fill my eyes.

I am lost in this pain, lost in this darkness

that lays trapped deep within my soul.

I cannot tell you that I will be okay.

I can only tell you

that if I see you tomorrow,

I survived another day.

I AM LOST

I have lost so much, that I don't know what to do anymore! I am stuck in this dark world that I live in and feel so totally confused within it all. How many times have I just sat here or just lie, staring into space. Into a black space, that seems to be the only thing that fills my life. Feeling worthless and lost. I have no idea what direction I am supposed to be heading in, or who I even am. I try to make sense of it all, but so much has happened and still happening that I do not know where I am meant to go! I keep hanging on, hoping to find my way through my pain and trauma of the darkness that lays buried within my weary bones. I feel like I have lost sight of who I am.

Lost in my thoughts to, that I can't work out how to move forward. It is like I don't belong. This journey I am on, seems to be an everlasting one, yet I never seem to get anywhere. Some days are truly harder than others and no matter if the sun beams through my open window first thing, it doesn't give me a burst of energy of wanting to get up and take my weary body out into the open air. Instead, I just lay slumped in a heap, waiting for the day to pass me by.

For so many years now, I have been this way. I don't know anymore, which direction I should be going, as I don't know where my life should be heading! My energy has been sucked from my once steady body, but now I am this weak soul who has completely lost her way! Trying so hard to find solid ground, but instead, my world is crumbling in front of me as I keep desperately looking for a connection that will lead me to the right path and get the right help in which to fill the cracks in my damaged life and restore my fragile frame, my broken soul.

I keep hurting and falling, even though I try so hard to keep digging, forming my own tracks, filling my own blank spaces, hoping to discover the right way to go. The right path for myself.

But I keep getting lost…

LOST SOUL

I am the one who has so much to say,

yet keep my words hidden

in the depths of my soul.

I carry my feelings

like a thousand waves,

in a state of hopelessness.

Deep within my tortured shell

is a pain that you will never know.

Locked inside my broken heart

where my weary soul resides.

I fight day and night

desperate to escape into the real world,

but instead, drown in my troubled mind,

lost in my own little world of darkness,

unsure of ever finding my rainbow

waiting on the other side.

I am just an empty shell…

A lost soul trying to find who I am.

SOUL IS LOST

I believe my journey in life since the 'abuse' was never meant to be simple, and it is why I feel as though part of me is not here and the part that is, is hanging by a thread. I no longer function, because I am not motivated, neither do I feel as though I have any control over what happens. I am disconnected from others and I cannot trust, because of what happened. I live fearing for my life, just about surviving. I hide away, shut myself off because it is my way of feeling safer. It is me against the world alone, only no one understands me because of what happened. I find it so difficult to even see a future! I ask myself all too often, who am I? Feeling alone and not even sure of what direction I should be going in, neither do I get what my purpose in life is anymore for it is like I don't belong and I am certainly not in control, hence why I try to detach myself from situations that live inside my head to try and protect myself. I sit and stare at empty spaces whilst I hide away in my darkness, because to me, I feel safer hiding behind my own walls, this is how I feel protected from fear.

I feel like I am on this journey, this long, never ending journey that seems to keep going only not actually leading to anywhere, never coming to a stop. A busy, busy world that has no place for this broken soul. No understanding of how I feel or how I need saving and as the seasons of life pass me by, the connection with my soul remains lost as I sit in a quiet spot, just listening to the birds' tones, taking in a gentle breeze, and watching the sun beam through the canopied trees, but I still hear the screaming thoughts that fill my head, as clear as symbols crashing, as the sound echoes within my restless being.

I try so hard to remove the high-pitched screeches that repeatedly fill my suffocating memories.

Every corner, every inch of my brain, drown with flashbacks, as my tears break from my eyes. So many scars, so many deep wounds that no one sees, embedded within my fragile frame as my now encrusted skin slowly burns away…

ALONE

There are no spaces for the light,

for it is the darkness that deeply entwines

through my body.

No place to hide, for my soul that is lost.

There is no hope

through the blackness of the dark shadows

that descend on my heart.

As piercing voices devour at my conscience

and insanity floods my insides.

No one sees my crumpled face

behind my mask,

trapped inside the prison of my mind.

No one sees my loneliness

that drains from my soul.

I live in fear…

I live in darkness…

I am alone.

BEING ALONE

I am on the brink of crying as I write this, because of my trauma and all that has happened since, I feel as though I am still trapped inside this prison of my mind. Right from the beginning, I believed it would be temporary, yet it feels like forever I have been like this. No-one sees how I live in fear, in darkness, because being alone is a situation. A hidden situation. Yes, I suffer and I hide it. I 'mask' my feelings. I pretend I am okay, but inside, I am hurting. More than you will ever know. While everyone is out there smiling and laughing with friends. I sit alone, trapped inside my body and the more I am by myself, the more I start to have thoughts that I don't belong!

Maybe I am better off being alone, isolating myself! I am better off hiding away and avoiding people, that way I can't get hurt again. I have been through enough trauma and I am still trying to process all my thoughts and emotions from what has happened. At least I feel safe in my own little bubble. At least I can sit with my own thoughts and without being judged. I feel 'safe' in my own setting. Whereas it is different outside. I 'fear' everything when I am outside or in surroundings that I am not familiar with.

I spend most of my time alone, at home, because that way I feel 'safe.' That way I can do what I want. If I want to sit in silence in a corner and cry, then I can. If I want to talk to my loved ones that are in another place, a beautiful world, then I can talk quietly to them. Being alone can be a lonely place to be sometimes. But I am content at being able to do what I want at the speed I want rather than have someone telling me what I should be doing. Yes. My mind may be forever going down a dark path. But, no one gets it anyway. Unless it has happened to them.

I am better off listening to my own voice echoing through empty walls, rather than people seeing the loneliness that drains from my soul.

Being alone, is the only way I can protect myself.

I LIVE IN DARKNESS

I live in the darkness of a black shadow

drowning in the waves of the ocean.

Icy winds fade to a gentle breeze

as the icicles like chandeliers

hang frozen in the night.

Spiralling into a world of doom

as pieces of my soul are scattered

and teardrops fall like tears

onto my broken skin.

A gown of emotions darkens my heart

as I continue to look for

the light in my world…

Hanging on to hope,

crying eternal notes of sadness.

DARK WORLD

(Trigger warning: This letter contains mention of suicide)

I am going to be honest and open here as painful as this is. Yes, I am suffering a great deal with my mental health and having the disorders I have is not always easy for people to understand or even get! I have a variety of disorders including PTSD, severe anxiety and depression and I have had to learn to live with my disorders, as hard as they are. I fight every day to try and get through the best I can, yet it feels like a constant torture. I feel lost and each moment that I live is an effort. It feels like my soul has been sucked out from a broken shell and I have been crushed into tiny little pieces and all the goodness and all the light has been drained from me and I am left totally alone in darkness. There is no path that leads me back to reality because the world to me just continues to be this huge dark space. It mentally and physically hurts and the saddest thing about this, is that no-one sees it. Neither do they see my tears because I hide them away. All they see is a smiling face of what they believe to be a strong person with confidence! They do not know of the dark world that I live in…

More than often, I have suicidal thoughts. I believe that the world would be better off without me in it, but I also look at it that I would be in a better place if I was no longer here. No more of this pain and suffering. No more fear. No more pretending. But instead, in a world of peace and love and kindness. Living in such a dark place. It is a place where I feel helpless. Where every day feels the same and time has no value. Throughout each day I feel numb and never quite sure how I am supposed to focus. It does take its toll on me and it is very hard to be able to get out of that place.

I have little faith in ever thinking I will see the light again because I feel trapped inside my head. It feels like nothing will help or ever change and what makes it even harder, is not being able to trust. I know a lot of people probably look at me and would not think for one minute that I felt this way. But that is the problem. No one sees what is underneath. No one sees what I am hiding. No one knows what I feel. It is so hard to believe that 'everything will ever be okay'!

TRAPPED

(Trigger Warning: This poem contains mention of abuse)

He sat beside me, and all I could hear was his heavy breath

but unable to see through the blindfold

that covered my tear- stained eyes.

My mouth forced shut, by the soiled cloth that filled my opening.

My lips blistered from the tape that bound them together.

My hands gauged from the tightening of the rope,

powerless to escape.

This was not going to end well…

I was terrified. He terrified me…

Silence surrounded me…

Until I heard his breath against my neck

as his fingers trailed the side of my face-

Slowly moving down…

A clenching around my throat from his cold hand.

Then two hands… As he tightened his grip-

I gasped for air…

Then I woke-

From the flashback that haunts me every night.

EVERY NIGHT

(Trigger Warning: This letter contains mention of abuse)

Haunted by this re- occurring flashback… Only this was real life many years ago and not a soul knows about it…This is the worst thing I have ever had to live through in my entire life. I am still trapped within the memory of what happened as I re live it every single night. He will never know that what he did was wrong. Neither will he ever be sorry. It is very hard for me to say what I went through, although the poem says it all and this letter will recapitulate what happened. This is someone I knew and I never thought that what he did to me would ever happen and believe me, none of you that are reading this will have any idea how hard it has been for me to write…

Just over 36 years ago I was abusively raped. Sexually, physically, psychologically, emotionally, violently, and viciously. My flashbacks every single night are the horrific memories of my trauma that he put me through and it feels like it is happening again and again. That night, he offered me a lift home, so I kindly accepted unaware of what was going to happen next! He drove to a dead-end road, apparently, he had to see a friend! The car stopped and within seconds he forced a soiled cloth into my mouth and taped it shut. I tried so hard to fight him off, but I wasn't strong enough and before I knew it, he had blindfolded my now tear stained eyes and tied my wrists together. I was trapped in this car, fearing for my life. This so-called friend, was some kind of monster that I did not recognize!! All I could hear was his heavy breath against my neck as his fingers trailed down the side of my cheek. I became more and more frightened, uncertain of how I was going to get away from him. Every night... I re- live it all. His breath upon me. What he did to me. Every night, I feel this and see this again and again.

Every night...I feel so scared, so anxious, so on edge like I cannot breathe. The intrusive thoughts and feelings fill me with panic. The vivid memories of that traumatic night continuously haunt me. So many questions I have asked myself over the years, yet I never have any answers. I am writing about my experience because I do not want to hide away anymore. I should not have to be made to feel guilty by writing this. By telling the world.

This is no dream.... This is no imagination... This is real....

RUN

(Trigger Warning: This poem contains mention of abuse)

Feelings of fear washed over me like a wave crashing on a shore.

Fear of the night ahead.

No light. Just complete darkness,

but I knew I had to take my chance

and run...

Breaking free from the rope that held my wrists together,

pulling the soiled cloth from my blistered mouth

and ripping at the tape.

I removed the dark stained blindfold

that was tight against my eyes and I ran…

Along muddy paths, through the silent woodland,

amongst the trees that filled the spaces in between.

My screams were not heard,

only by the demon that chased me

as I became trapped in a dead end.

His voice whispered…

"THERE IS NOWHERE TO RUN…THERE IS NO ESCAPE

FEAR OF THE UNKNOWN

(Trigger Warning: This letter contains mention of abuse)

I heard him get out of the car, but I did not hear him lock the doors! I knew this was my only chance to escape, but I also knew I was risking my life, as I did not know if he was even waiting outside the car, or if he had gone to get his friend, so I did not have time to waste. I had somehow with my elbow, managed to lift the handle of the door and quietly nudged it open and pushed it gently, still not knowing of his whereabouts! As I twisted my hands, the more I was able to loosen the rope that held my wrists together. I pushed the door open being as quiet as I possibly could and ran, ripping at the blindfold that was now soaked from my tear-stained eyes and tugged at the tape that held my lips shut and pulling the soiled cloth from my mouth, and I ran. It was now or never, so I ran as fast as my weak legs could take me. Pulling the remainder of the rope from my wrists as I ran and ran and ran and ran. I had no idea where I was or where I was heading for, but I just knew I had to escape from him…There was no sign of a road just muddy footpaths that led through a woodland. I continued running, constantly looking over my shoulder. I hoped so much, that I would come to a road at the end. But the more I ran, the deeper into the woodland I seemed to go. Until there was nowhere… Nowhere else to run to. Complete darkness closed in around me and suddenly I heard footsteps and heavy breathing getting closer. It had to be him…

All that surrounded me were trees. Hundreds of them. I could not recognize this huge, never-ending forest. I just knew I was so scared amongst the blackness that suffocated me.

I tried so hard to keep on running, deeper and deeper in amongst the canopies that interlinked with one and other, hoping to find a way out at the other end, but his footsteps got closer and closer until I could run no more. He had reached me and he was not going to let me go. I knew then that there was no escaping from him as he pushed me down to the ground. I tried so hard to fight my way from his grip, believing I was about to take my last breath. Believing I was going to die.

I am forever in the same place and the exact same vivid flashback night after night. Nothing changes. Because of that 'demon' I live in fear. Fear of the 'unknown.'

AS I DIE ALONE

(Trigger Warning: This poem contains mention of abuse)

Black is the world that surrounds me

in the silence of the night.

A world of endless fear-

My eyes covered by his one hand

as the other claw at my motionless body

as he presses against my skin,

pushing me down into the hole beneath me.

Panic fills my lungs as I fight to breathe, gasping for air…

Struggling to free myself from the fear that holds me trapped.

My hands reach out for help,

but the grip only tightens around my throat

as it squeezes every drop of air from me.

Submerged into the ground below as fear crushes my bones…

Gulping for one last breath,

concealed from sight.

Alone beneath the hidden brambles.

No-one can save me now.

As here I wait … to die.

IT HAPPENED TO ME

(Trigger Warning: This letter contains mention of abuse and suicide)

The night was silent, all but the heavy breathing coming from the 'demon.' He pushed me down onto the ground and after kicking me several times, he forced himself inside me. I fought so hard to escape his grip but his hands tightened around my neck as I gulped for one last breath as I submerged into the ground further, knowing that no one was going to save me. Nobody even knew I was here, so how could I possibly be saved? I honestly believed at that precise moment, that I was going to die. He thought it was funny when I begged him to stop, as tears fell from my eyes. I kept saying no, I kept saying stop, but his hand tightened over my mouth. He never stopped. I had wished so much in that moment that I was dead because I was so scared.

It has been 36 years of suffering, still terrified. I have become a prisoner in my own mind because of what that 'demon' did. I can't undo what he did, but I can speak out of how he has destroyed my life...My world ended that night and ever since, I have attempted to end my life because I have wanted to be rid of the pain and fear I feel. I am constantly thinking about what happened. I want to escape from the overwhelming distress I am in, that fills my head now and for all the years I have not told a soul. Having it eat away at me, day by day. Night by night...It has been torturing keeping this quiet, pretending I am okay. Knowing that not a soul has any idea what I have been through or even still going through. It feels like my heart has been ripped out and still I live this horrific journey, trapped in this dark secret.

For a while, I wasn't sure whether to write this or even have published, but I asked myself over and over, why should I keep suffering in silence…

Not anymore. It is no longer a secret…. Now I am telling the world. But what he did, will always be with me.

EVERLASTING TERROR

(Trigger Warning: This poem contains mention of abuse)

My night is restless as I suffer in this everlasting torment.

Where piercing eyes look down intensely at my fragile body

as I try to shield myself from this figure.

Whilst memories close in and the cold,

black fear draws towards me…

My eyes shut tight from what leers over my startled frame,

but my ears listen to the heavy breaths from the dark demon.

Hands engage grabbing at my throat,

as I gasp for air desperate to be freed…

My clothes ripped from my now battered body

as he forces himself upon me.

Where the night turns blacker, whilst my crying grows louder

and I stay curled in this fragile state,

wishing for this night to end.

Paralyzed, in this night of fear,

trying to contain my thoughts in silence.

I simply wait…in hope,

that I awaken from this darkness-

This everlasting terror.

WILL I EVER ESCAPE?

(Trigger Warning: This letter contains mention of abuse)

That night…

I tried so desperately to get away. I attempted to cry out for help, I tried so hard, but as one hand covered my mouth, the other tightened itself around my throat, striking me repeatedly as he continued to violently abuse my fragile body as I submerged further into the ground. I was trapped underneath him, but I kept trying to push him off me, crying and begging him to stop. I was so frightened that he might kill me, so I didn't want to make him angry.

What felt like forever and fearing for my life, a flicker of light appeared in the distance as if someone was shining a bright torch! But whatever it was, it startled the 'demon.' He lifted his body from mine and kicked me several times before running off. Here I was alone and scared. Battered and bruised in the middle of nowhere in this dark hole. I lay there for what felt like forever, feeling dirty and shocked at what just happened, but grateful that I was still alive. I never did see where the light was coming from, but it shone long enough for me to find my way out from the woodland that surrounded me. Then as quick as it had appeared it was gone. Wherever it came from, it saved my life that night. Somehow, I made my way home and once inside I found I was alone. I destroyed the clothes in which I had been wearing. Showered and covered the marks and bruises on my face and legs as I fell to the floor and sobbed my heart out, realizing what had

46

just happened. I was viciously, violently raped by someone that I believed to be a friend. I thought he was going to kill me. I thought it was the end for me.

I have flashbacks again and again about the whole incident of what happened and what I keep fearing will happen again…This same 'demon' haunts me every single night. Every night I fear as I try to bury myself under the covers in hope that it will go away. But it stays in my head, it is like it takes over my mind. I am too scared to go out for walks in broad daylight because I believe everywhere I go; everybody is going to hurt me.

It is like I am living the moment all over again. I am paralyzed by the fear wondering if this will ever go away. If there will ever be an escape…

DEMON

(Trigger Warning: This poem contains mention of abuse)

In silence… I wait…

No escape. No place to hide.

Alone… All alone.

I feel I no longer exist

within this stillness of darkness of mist.

Enshrouded trees like ghosts,

bracken bent.

Just waiting now…

To walk free

from this everlasting torment.

Lying here and listening

to the cries of my soul,

for the return of the 'demon'

in which I have no control.

But from my sight he has slid away

to hide, until some other day.

THIS DEMON

(Trigger Warning: This letter contains mention of abuse)

He is the one that continues to return to my head again and again as I re-live that night. The 'demon' that abusively raped me. There is no warning, just vivid memories of my traumatic time that he put me through, but it feels like it is happening now. Every sound, every smell. I hear it all. I feel it all. I smell it all…. Every second that he put me through. He did not stop that night. He violently tore me apart. Broke me. Battered me. But it wasn't just what he did to me physically, it was the pain inside. The unseen pain. I cried so much that night. I still cry now. It is easy for people to say 'this is not happening now; it is in the past.' But when you have faced such a traumatic time in your life, it is not a case of just getting over it. It stays with you. It eats away at you… It is called PTSD. I have kept this hidden. I have lived with this for over 36 years and I am still re-living it and yes, this is something that happened a long time ago, but I still have triggers that put me back in that place. Whether it be people or situations or thoughts, emotions, sensations even flashbacks of images of what happened of where I was. I can be fine one minute then 'bang,' I am straight back there again.

I live in fear that what the 'demon' did to me will happen again. I refuse to go anywhere on my own, because I am so scared someone is going to follow me. Even when I go to bed, I fear someone is going to get into my home. I am paranoid every single day that something bad is going to happen. He has destroyed my life. I have spent years living with this in secret, living constantly in fear of it happening again.

The 'demon' that brutally raped me comes into my head every single night. I tried so hard to get away, endless times, the night it happened and here I am re living all that he did to me. That night changed my life forever and I feel so angry with myself for not getting him locked away, like he so deserved. I want people to know the reality of 'rape.' It does happen and I for one feel that this is where I not only speak out for what happened to me, but for all the women that read this that may have already sadly gone through the same thing. Don't hide away like me…. Do not remain silent….

Report it….

NO ESCAPE

(Trigger Warning: This poem contains mention of abuse)

I am awake…

In which I live through most nights.

Where there is no escape

and there are no lights.

Where there are no voices,

only the one that screams my name.

It haunts me each night,

it is for real it is no game

I come to an end and I feel myself fall,

unable to breathe, I attempt to call.

Scared and alone, I hear footsteps behind

as I reach a dead end at the path in my mind.

Year after year I have suffered in silence

my life in ruins due to this 'demons' violence.

These flashbacks that I live through

are the night of the rape.

Forever in my head, there is

'No escape'

HE THOUGHT IT WAS OKAY TO DO WHAT HE DID

(Trigger Warning: This poem contains mention of abuse)

June 1987 was the date I was brutally, violently, viciously raped. Just 21 years old. There are reasons why I have never said anything. Mainly, for not being believed, especially after the person I did tell, made me feel as though it was my fault! Neither did I have the courage to tell my family because I was too scared of what that vicious 'demon' would do to me again. From the day it happened, I pushed it all to the back of my mind. For a while, I believed it had left my head, but how wrong was I. It had not left at all. Detail for detail of what he did to me that night was still in my mind and that was when I realized that it was never going to go away. To him, it meant absolutely nothing. He thought it was okay to do what he did, but for me, it has affected my life ever since. I have had to live with this trauma. It has destroyed my life and still does. Re-living this torture in my head, again and again, like it is happening for real. Every single detail. Every sound. Every smell. He thought it was okay to do what he did, however much I begged for him to stop.

I pleaded so much that night for him to stop, but he kept on taking, he kept on breaking me. I remember being so, so scared as he forced himself upon me, taking every inch of me. His fingers scraping my skin, making me bleed, then punching my fragile body without hesitation. He did not stop. He wouldn't stop. I tried so hard to scream

54

out, but his hand continuously suffocated my mouth, drowning any noise that I attempted to let out....

That night, he broke me in so many ways and as well as taking my trust in men, he has scared me to the point of not wanting to go out alone. This was never my fault.... But the 'demon' who did this to me. He thought it was okay to do what he did, but it wasn't. He has destroyed me. He has destroyed my life. Whilst writing this now even, it makes me realize just how alone I have been for the last 36 years. Not being able to be open about this! But, because this happened to me, because what 'he' did to me, it has made me realize I have had to write this in my book. This is for every woman that has been through the same as me...

Do not remain silent. It is time to break that silence.

LET ME BE FREE

(Trigger Warning: This poem contains mention of abuse)

Let me be free…

From this demon that haunts me

in my world of struggle.

The darkness within my shattered soul

just waiting to break out.

Laying broken and twisted,

clinging on to hope.

Let me be free…

From this terrifying ordeal

that I live every single night.

As the memories take over

in my messed- up head,

splintering my heart as I suffer in silence.

Re-living that night…

His hands engulfing me in his clutches,

beating me, raping me,

my tears falling down my cheeks, begging for him to stop.

Let me be free…

Do not let this be the end for me!

I WANT TO BE FREE

(Trigger Warning: This contains mention of rape)

How do you recover from a brutal rape when you have not spoken about it to anyone? I have held on to this for so long and it has stopped me from regaining any sense of control or self- worth, neither have I been able to heal. I want to stop feeling scared and alone. I want the flashbacks to go away. I want to stop living in fear. I was petrified of the outcome if I had told anyone about that night…. I even had to destroy my clothes after it happened, instead of taking them to the police, because looking at them, put me into a major panic attack and reminded me repeatedly about what that 'demon' did to me and I feared him coming for me again! But, because of my silence, this has had a power over me for all these years. It has shattered my sense of security and safety, making me feel helpless in what I believe to be a dangerous world. Unable to trust other people. I do not believe I ever will! This has lived with me for this long now and I honestly think it will always be with me. Every night I bury my head under my cover because I am so scared the 'demon' is in the room and is going to rape me again. I still feel his hands around my throat. I still feel him forcibly thrusting himself into me and I wake up with so many bruises and scratches on my body, having no idea how they got there! I must grab at myself in fear, believing it is happening all over again. I see him in my head and most nights I wake up screaming as I feel a tightness closing in over my mouth like I can't breathe, believing I am going to die like I thought I was the night it happened. The night he raped me. The night he took my life. All I want now is to be 'free' from this. I want to stop living in fear. I want to have help in making sense of my feelings that I have carried for so many years. To be free from the flashbacks I live through every single day and night that frighten me so much. I no longer want to be living this life of fear and isolation. I trusted him, because he was a friend and all I have kept asking myself is should I have! He abusively raped me. Viciously and violently. He has done this to me. He has made me not trust anyone, not feel safe wherever I go or wherever I am. To feel threatened by anyone I see. He has caused me to have PTSD, to feel anxious and depressed. To continuously re live what happened. To be petrified of the slightest thing. Panicked, overwhelmed, and frightened that what he did is going to happen again. I do not want to be like this anymore. I want to be free.

DEMON WITHIN ME

(Trigger Warning: This poem contains mention of abuse)

There is a demon within me

that controls my mind

as he drains the light from my eyes

and rips my soul apart.

In this black space of endless fear

the coldness rears its ugly head

dragging me to the depths of hollowness.

His eyes burning deeply into the darkness

of my soul, as he comes

tearing at my inner self.

Carves away at me with his scarred hands-

Suffocating my screams…

Save me…please save me

from this demon that lives within me,

in the dark, twisted corners of my mind…

INSIDE MY MIND

My mind is full of so many things, mainly bad thoughts, because I have had to live my life holding everything inside, keeping quiet, not wanting to tell anyone how I am feeling. I wish every day, that these horrid thoughts and feelings would go away and that it will get easier. But it doesn't and I know, that unless I can talk about it, it will just get worse and worse until I get to the point where I break…. My mind is surrounded by so much negativity that I can never imagine identifying a positive mind ever again! It is said, 'time heals all wounds' but I believe that there are some things that you just cannot get over. I have felt very much alone in my life, because I have held this secret for so long, holding on to so many tears and other times I have screamed them out.

How much longer will I be hostage within these chains that hold me captive inside my mind? When will I get to break free from my wounded life that I have clung to for so long? I fight my lonely battles every day and night, that not a single person sees, even the memories that I try so hard to erase, continue to haunt me again and again, as they keep on trampling my now suffering soul. My bones crumbling into dust, my thoughts spiralling amongst my haunting cries, as darkness swallows me whole. How much longer will I live these lonely battles inside my mind, and these racing, uncontrollable thoughts that tug on my frail heart, silently stirring in my soul. I cannot concentrate. I cannot relax. I cannot sleep because the demon is inside my mind re-playing what happened. I so wish I could turn the switch off in my head.

That demon has done this to me. He controls my mind. Even now, after all these years, he still has control over me. Even now, I weep beneath the wild sky that hangs over me, as I lie in darkness. My soul tired as it spirals in this world of hurt as he continues to live inside my mind…

MEMORY

(Trigger Warning: This poem contains mention of abuse)

In my head there is a memory

of the most damaging abuse I have ever encountered.

From a time when I believed I was to blame.

A dreaded secret I refused to share with anyone.

A memory that has stuck in my head,

smothering my soul as I drown in my tears.

Of a dark, cold night in the middle of nowhere.

No one to protect me. No one to save me.

How many broken tears fell that night?

How many times did I plead?

A memory in my head

that constantly reminds me of that silent night.

That 'demon' that I knew,

left me damaged, broken and scarred for life.

In my head, there is a memory of a time that once was

yet still, it keeps on haunting me,

overwhelming me with sheer terror

of another vicious attack. A memory in my head…

That will stay with me forever.

WITH ME FOREVER

(Trigger Warning: This letter contains mention of abuse)

A memory that is still destroying me repeatedly. I have sunk to depths that have had me wondering if I would ever be able to get out from. Tormented by this evilness that continues to eat away at me, as I struggle to find some peace within. Will this ever let me forget? Ever let me move on? Or will it be with me forever?

 It took a lot for me to go to who I trusted would believe me and understand, but instead, they made me feel as though I was some erratic, mad woman. After that, I thought my chances of seeing justice were non-existent so I walked away. I wanted so much to tell my mum, my best friend, what really happened that night, but I was afraid that the demon would find out I had already told someone and that he would come after me, again. Instead, I have lived trapped by that monster. The monster that changed my life forever and I knew I had to somehow get on with my life. It is 36 years now and this is 'me' talking about it. I tell you this has affected me in so many ways. Making me feel like I do not belong. I want the world to know that I am sharing this with all of you now because I feel I need to. I do not want to be silent anymore. I want to speak out. What he did to me has made me live in fear. The continuous flashbacks I have that make me believe I am back in that moment. Back in that car, tied up, blindfolded, and gagged. Running for my life in pitch black, not knowing where I was. Beaten viciously, brutally raped, and then left for dead. My body and mind scarred for life. Every man I see, unless I know them well, is a potential rapist in my eyes. I am unable to trust just anyone, because all I see is 'rapist' in them. The flashbacks, the images, the emotions, the memory… Whether I am awake or asleep, it feels as though I am right there again in that moment. I was subjected to the worst form of abuse and violence and I am reminded every single day and night of what he did to me. I live in constant fear with anxiety and despair and mistrust everyone because my head is full of negative thoughts that chip away at my insides.

I do not want to live in this darkness anymore. I do not want to be a victim, but I know that this will be a memory that will stay with me forever…

LIVING

(Trigger Warning: This poem contains mention of abuse)

Sometimes I shed tears not because I am sad,

but because I am scared.

So scared...

These feelings that nobody understands.

Because in that moment I do not know who I am.

The intrusive flashbacks where I am awake

where there is no escape...

Where the demon continues to abusively rape me,

viciously, mentally, physically, and emotionally destroy me.

I need help, but where do I start,

when my head is filled with fear,

dragging me to the depths of hollowness.

Screaming out to be heard…

Only my voice echoes

through the empty walls.

Here I am hanging on to hope,

trying to do this thing called 'living.'

It is not because I cannot let go of the past,

but because the past will not let go of me.

LIVING THIS EVERY DAY

(Trigger Warning: This letter contains mention of abuse and suicide)

It is so hard to go on living when I have had such a traumatic time happen to me in my lifetime. The immense suffering, it has destroyed me, and still feels as if the whole world is crashing down on my weak and troubled body, tearing away at my soul, making it impossible to continue with life. Living there in that moment, where I cling to the memories of what happened, makes it impossible to be able to move forward. I feel angry, upset, anxious, scared, panicked, on edge. I am bruised, broken, and scarred. Being a victim of abuse has been the cause of my mental health disorders and all too often I get fed up with people making me feel as though I have nothing wrong with me. My feelings and what happened to me are real and people should not say anything about something they do not know about. No one knows what happened to me or what I went through and still going through and how destroyed I am. I have been professionally diagnosed with PTSD and this is going to be with me for the rest of my life.

I avoid loud noises that are likely to trigger my trauma and places where there are lots of people. All too often I avoid going out altogether, as I am afraid something will happen to me because the flashbacks are such vivid memories of what happened and I live in fear that it is going to happen again. Just the slightest sound, sight or smell can bring on an attack, giving me the illusion that I am back in that place I was before. Scared and fearing for my life.

Things that I used to look upon as simple are now extremely difficult, even impossible. It feels like this has been a lifelong impact, but I know now that I am mentally ill and all because of the 'demon' that has destroyed me. He has left me to carry what happened to me, what he did, leaving me weak, taking every little piece of my fragile body.

I believe there is no right way or wrong way in which I should be dealing with this although I know I need the help of professional people to process all that I am going through.

I want to let go of the past, but the past just will not let go of me…

I CANNOT LET HIM WIN

I know that trying to live every day

with that memory in my head-

That constant fear,

the forever questions that will not leave my mind.

Always believing that it was my fault…

I lost myself, in the silence of that night.

There are no words, for he brutally struck me,

he scarred me.

I am still there…

Drowning with emotion.

My piercing screams and haunting dreams

hanging on to the fragile threads of my life.

There have been times I thought

I would never make it.

But I have, somehow

and now… I must hold on.

However painful my memory is.

I cannot let him take over my life, any longer.

I cannot let him win.

STILL HOLDING ON

(Trigger Warning: This letter contains mention of abuse)

Even now, the 'demon' still comes to me in my everyday living making me feel that nowhere is safe and that I cannot trust anyone, which has a significant impact on my daily life causing me a variety of symptoms, making me avoid situations, people, and places. My life feels unsafe, leaving me feeling scared, and alone. Plagued by frightening memories. The world just feels like an unsafe place to be and I always have this sense that something bad is going to happen to me again and that I have no way of protecting myself. I try so hard to fight it, to survive, but I become overwhelmed by what is going on, I freeze in fear. So many times, I just want to run. Run from everything. The dark thoughts that continue to haunt me every single day and night. To escape from all that continue to drown my mind. But it is not that easy, it is never that easy, because I am carrying this emotional, fearful, baggage of negativity each day. I spend so many days and nights crying, barely hanging on, that I can't eat or sleep, when really, I just want to be able to go outside and reconnect with the world, to be free from all that keeps holding me back. To feel safe. I don't know where I belong anymore! But I do know, I am struggling to untangle myself from the different emotions in which I am feeling.

How dare this 'demon' make such a brutal attack on me and make me live with this for so long not telling a soul. He has got away with it, whilst I have had to live all these years with this secret… The truth is,

I have had to live fearing for my life every single day since that brutal rape. No one knowing about it, but me.

But not anymore. I am admitting to the torture he put me through that night. You have all heard it here first, in my book.

Here I am still holding on....

REALITY

My life has taught me…

That I have lost myself.

I am trapped in a world that has destroyed me.

I have suffered and I have lost hope.

It is like all my pieces have been swept away

and the ones that are left do not seem to fit anymore.

I try to keep myself safe… Hidden from the world.

But I am alone and sad. I am helpless-

I continue to walk my path of brokenness,

numb from the pain burning through my veins,

tormented by the memories I wish I

could erase from my mind.

I will keep on reaching out-

As I try to find a reason for me to exist

whilst telling myself...

This is my reality.

MY REAL LIFE

The world can feel like a very dark place living with both mental health and physical health disorders and all too often I have little hope for things ever feeling better. It is very challenging and overwhelming and a lot of the time, unbearable. I never imagined that I could ever feel like this and doing absolutely nothing about it! It has been an incredibly lonely experience, where so many bad and painful things have happened and I have had to live with them for so long. My conditions affect my everyday life, from having no motivation, to my overall wellbeing, to my negative thinking, the changes in my mood and struggling to cope. I believe my life is full of darkness that has taken over my body and I am just not able to erase it and although I try so hard to find a way to cope with it; instead, I carry all that continues to make me fear the world and fear all the obstacles I must deal with. I believe this is how my life is going to be forever.

There are so many times when I feel as though I am suffocating. Fighting so many battles in my mind and I try so hard to escape from my tangled-up thoughts, but my brain just doesn't let me break free. Instead, I continue falling and falling, deeper into the depths of blackness that fill the hole below my shivering body. I try so hard to get out from what claws at my broken skin, but the walls continue to cave in, challenging my weakened self.

People do not see what my real life is because I hide it well. It is like when someone says to me 'how are you?' I always answer with 'I am okay thank you' even though it is very far from the truth. But one, I do not want to have to admit to someone that I am struggling and two, I do not want that someone to have to feel as though they must deal with my problems. Reality is hard because I cannot acknowledge what is real when I have had such traumatic things happen to me in my life. I believe that all that has happened, is how it will always be. Because, whatever I focus my attention on, becomes my reality.

Maybe I am trapped. Maybe, I just cannot escape from this world that I live in. The continuous negative thoughts, the continuous pain. Maybe this life I live is the only life I know!

HIDDEN SECRET

(Trigger Warning: This poem contains mention of rape)

Hidden secret...

Because only I knew the truth.

Until now.

Of course, I am sorry that I had to let him go,

but how could I possibly keep him,

and why should I be made to feel guilty.

I never asked for this to happen.

Why would I want to be forever reminded

of the abusive rape that 'demon' put me through.

The day he was born, I was not even able to look at him,

but I heard his cries, his screams, until they took him away.

I cried so many tears myself that day and for many days after.

It was never his fault, but it was never mine either.

All I hope is that he has lived his life, lived it well…

Still living it, wherever he is.

I hope he forgives me for letting him go.

Because of that 'demon' I could not keep him.

I am sorry….

I HAD TO LET HIM GO

(Trigger Warning: This letter contains mention of rape)

I have been sitting for hours, trying to find the words to write this letter. Trying to find the right words that mean exactly what I am thinking. How do I write about a child that has been a hidden secret for over 36 years! No one knows the truth, but will find out now....

I am sorry that I could not be his mum, but I am sure his new parents would have given him the best start in life and even the best future he could ever want.

To find out I was expecting a baby, should have been the happiest moment of my life. But it was not for me. Not this time.

Five months had passed since that horrific night where I was brutally raped and battered. Left for dead and here I was, pregnant and too late to do anything about it. I never found out until it was way too late. The nine months came around and a baby boy was born. I never even saw him, but I heard his cries and screams until they took him away, because I could not keep him. How could I? Every time I would look at him, I would be reminded of what that evil 'demon' did to me. He will probably never know where he came from or ever know the living hell I went through, or the memory I have had to carry for so many years.

I know, as he grows up, he will always wonder why I had to give him away and I know he will never get to hear the truth unless he was to hear it from me. I had to do it, I had to do what was best. The decision I made was the right decision.

I know it was not his fault and I would never blame that poor, innocent child, but all I can hope is that if he ever learns of the truth of what happened to me, he will forgive me for not keeping him. I hope that he will look at it that I gave him a chance. I gave him life. Even though it was never with me, he has had a life. He has lived. I gave him that chance.

TO YOU, THE DEMON

I know that you would never be sorry

and I know that you would never admit to what you did.

There were times I felt I would never make it…

Yet here I am still fighting each day.

You may have destroyed me, you may have broken me,

you may have silenced me for so long

and the memories left behind will always haunt me.

But I do not want to be the person

that you have made me become-

Not anymore.

I want to live my life without you keeping on

pushing in to my head and taking over.

Destroying me.

So, I have now been open to everyone

I have told the world now…

They all know what you did,

they all know what you are.

You are the 'Demon' that has destroyed my life.

LEAVE ME BE

(Trigger Warning: This letter contains mention of rape and suicide)

I knew you. You were a friend. Or so I thought! I have tried so hard to forget, but that night was the darkest and loneliest night I have ever felt in my life and I have had to live with that ever since. I remember every single detail as if it has just happened and I have had to try so hard to cope with this trauma ever since and believe me, it does not get any easier because I live my life now, in fear. I feel sick, even now, writing this and guilty for not saying anything to my family or friends at the time. But you made me like this. You made me this victim, having to suffer in silence. You are the 'demon' that sexually, physically, mentally, psychologically, emotionally, and verbally abused me. You raped me. You got me pregnant. You violated my body. You have broken me. You have stripped me of the person I once was, and because of you, I am not the person I want to be. You have been destroying me for over 36 years now and I want you gone. Gone from my mind. Gone from my flashbacks. Gone from my memory... Leave me to move on in my life, to deal with my every day being. Let me think about other things without you keeping on pushing in and taking over. I am trying so hard to live my life. I am trying so hard to grieve for my loved ones. Trying so hard to forget what you did, but you just keep coming back. Leave me be...NOW. Get out of my head, because I do not want to keep remembering what you did to me that night. I am exhausted and I do not want to live with this anymore. The painfulness of what you did to me. No matter how much I cried and screamed, you never stopped. Instead, you carried on hurting me violently, and viciously. I have been trying so hard to move on from you but you continue to destroy my life. I have kept you secret for so many years, and living with this has been impossible because you keep haunting me repeatedly. Eating away at me, breaking me down. Because of you…. I want to die.

Wherever you are, I hope every day, that you remember what you did to me and I hope that you are haunted by the violence that you put upon me. I hope that right from that night and for the rest of your life, you will never forget, because I haven't and I never will.

LIVING WITH MY MENTAL HEALTH DISORDERS

(Trigger Warning: This poem contains mention of suicide and death)

I try to hide from the unknown.

I feel that something is inside me trying to escape me.

I wait… I must simply wait, in hope that I will not fade

within the darkness of feeling trapped within myself.

A world of anxiety- Haunted by memories of my past.

Suicide is my answer, many times I have tried.

If only they knew! How many tears I have cried.

They tell me to get over it-

'Get over it' everyone says-

How I wish I could chase away all the bad things in my head

and stop wishing every day that I was dead.

If only they knew, that I want these feelings to stop.

To be myself again, for my heart to mend.

To be able to look to the future.

Instead of 'the end.'

MY MENTAL HEALTH DISORDERS

My conditions affect my every day thinking, feeling, my mood and behaviour. They can come on sudden, they can last for a short period or they can last for a very long time. They can affect the way in which I function, also how I relate to others. My mental health disorders make my life difficult. They are not a weakness but rather what is happening to me and around me and the worst part of all is that nobody knows how I am truly feeling unless I tell them. I have had to learn to live with my disorders and I fight every single day to try and live a normal life. Whatever normal is! I am lost in the darkness that surrounds me as the tears fall from my eyes as I desperately search for a way out from what suffocates me daily....

Living in fear of not knowing if what I went through is likely to ever happen again. It is so hard to be able to trust anyone, having spent my life looking over my shoulder and asking myself who I can trust and who I can't. It is not nice having to live in fear because I have had to become aware of my existence being in danger and I no longer feel as though I am the one in control. The nightmares might never go away and the fear of being around people that I do not know, or in this case, even those that I do know, may always be with me. Having mental health disorders makes me see the world in a different way. I see things that others do not see. I notice the emptiness in people's eyes because it is the same emptiness that I hold in mine. I see the fake smiles, the anxiety they feel. I see all this, because they are the same as me. I look at my life the way it is, with the clouding emotions that pull at my heart every day. There is no happiness. This will always be a battle that I will have to keep fighting. A battle of darkness. A battle of dark thoughts that take over my mind and control my life. It may just be that I will always be like this. It might make it impossible for me to ever feel any different.

I cannot change ME, but I will keep hanging on to hope ….

EVERY DAY

Miserable

Emotional

Nightmares

Trauma

Aches and pains

Lack of sleep

Hopelessness

Exhausted

Anxious

Low Moods

Trouble Focusing

Helpless

Disturbing Flashbacks

Isolated

Sad

Overdosing thoughts

Re-living traumatic event

Depressed

Everlasting Trauma

Restless

Suicidal

THESE ARE MY MENTAL HEALTH DISORDERS

(Trigger Warning: This letter contains mention of suicide)

Truth be said, I have struggled with my mental health for many years, yet never told a soul. It is not that easy to expose my feelings and thoughts. I guess I have never wanted to come across as 'weak.' So many people suffer with their mental health, but in my case, it is a disorder that I have. Mental health and mental health illnesses/disorders are quite often used as meaning the same, but they are not. Lots of people have mental health, especially in the world we live in. But not everyone has a mental illness/disorder. Mine, are something that affects the way I think, behave, and even interact. Having been diagnosed with PTSD, severe depression, and anxiety, I must cope with all the above every single day of my life and even when tears roll down these cheeks of mine, no matter how hard I try, I just cannot stop them. I try to hold my emotions inside most of the time, because on many occasions, I have been told I over react! Sadly, some people just don't get it, do they? The thing is, this makes me a whole lot worse as I then feel as though I am trapped inside my own body, trying so hard to get out, screaming to be set free. I should not be told that I must hold my emotions inside. Why should I have to? I cannot control how my emotions work! I cannot help the way I am! I have a major difficulty with trusting people in this world as it is, that I don't need to be told I am over reacting. My disorders are an illness and they make me feel sad and worried as it is. No one has any idea how scared I get, to the point where I cannot control my suicidal thoughts, and if I feel I want to end my life, you know something? I will just go ahead and do it.

I sometimes imagine my life as a picture in a frame. It would not be a 'picture of perfection,' that is for sure- More like an outline of my life, a blurred vision! Dark lines with gaps in between. Spaces where fear rolls into panic and pieces of my soul are shattered around the edges of the frame that is broken in so many places. My life all over, every single day. This is a picture of my mental health disorders, that reflects so much sadness…

So much of the 'true' me.

MY PTSD

(Trigger Warning: This poem contains mention of intrusive thoughts)

Do you have any idea how hard it is when you have intrusive thoughts
in your head

but have no way of getting them out in the open-

This is me.

I want to scream 'help' in hope that someone will hear me

as tears stream down my face. But no one hears...

I am trying to find a way out of a dark hole, with no light to help guide
me.

Traumatic flashbacks that replay over and over in my head.

Having the worst thoughts ever and repetitive images.

Screaming out, but no one hears...

There are so many times where I just want to shout out 'I'm
drowning.'

Drowning in my pain of fear, broken into a thousand pieces-

Trying so hard to survive but instead, lost in this journey of mine.

Battered and torn, empty and hopeless, feeling permanently worthless.

Do you have any idea how hard it is?

To have to face this all alone, even when I am so desperate,

when I need someone to listen, to help, to understand.

I try so hard to say how I feel,

but no one hears....

PTSD FOR ME

(Trigger Warning: This letter contains mention of suicide)

PTSD is post-traumatic stress disorder. It is caused by experiencing, seeing, or hearing a single event or multiple events that are traumatic. Although I have lived with it for many, many years, my PTSD was not diagnosed until 2017 because I never said a word to anyone about how I was feeling and sadly, it took for me to take an overdose before I was properly diagnosed. PTSD for me is distressing memories, nightmares/flashbacks, and racing thoughts about what happened to me and re-living the experience which cause overwhelming emotions, such as feeling negatively about myself and feeling on edge all the time. I re-live my traumatic event every single day and night, through vivid flashbacks and distressing images with intense, disturbing thoughts and feelings. I suffer with night sweats, shakes, panic attacks and easily scared and startled, overly sensitive to things such as noise and smells. It is like the trauma is happening right now which makes me feel irritable, anxious, sad, angry, but also guilty for not saying a word to anyone. I isolate myself because I am too afraid to go to places. Places that are filled with so many people. People that I do not know and constantly looking over my shoulder in fear that I am being followed. The world to me seems as though it is not a safe place to be because I am unable to trust anyone. I barely sleep, because the constant flashbacks suffocate my head every single night. If I am honest, I am scared to go to sleep because everything feels so real, like it is happening all over again. I lose control of my emotions, from being angry to sad to depressed to suicidal thoughts, feeling completely hopeless because I think I will never change and that things will never get better. PTSD is not something that I can just get over or forget. It is not something just made up, neither is it an excuse. It is living in a constant nightmare. PTSD is not just about worrying what might happen next, it is remembering what did happen! I am always so sorry for how I have been and how I am and what this is doing to me. It is not okay to say I need to learn how to overcome my distressing symptoms and to move beyond my traumatic experience. It is not that easy to just regain my life. I need professional help and I am not afraid to admit it. Not ever.

ANXIETY/PANIC

(Trigger Warning: This poem contains mention of anxiety and panic)

I cannot breathe…

My heart pounding,

darkness closing in on this fragile body.

Shaking, sweating…suffocating.

Confined within this solitary zone.

My inner self broken,

longing to break the chains that hold me captive.

Darkness entraps my weary body

in its entangling web.

Lying trapped within my screaming self,

trying so hard to escape.

Panic, worry, fear

closing in around me.

Pounding, racing heart.

Sweating, trembling, shaking

desperate to break free…

To break free from this

anxiety this panic,

that is closing in around me…

WHAT IS ANXIETY/PANIC FOR ME?

(Trigger Warning: This letter contains mention of anxiety and panic symptoms)

A lot of people do not understand the reality behind anxiety/panic and one of the hardest things about suffering from it, is the lack of understanding from others.

I get myself in such a state for the slightest thing and immediately think the worst. There is never a set time for an attack. It can just happen, and when it does it is the worst feeling because I have no control over it. It is real. The symptoms are real.

When I have an anxiety attack, it is usually triggered by certain things. Particularly about things that are about to happen or which I think are going to happen, which is why I avoid situations that might cause me to feel anxious. Where I have a disorder, this does not go away because I get an ongoing feeling of dread which affects my daily life, including feeling stressed and on edge, aches and pains, difficulty controlling my feelings of worry and fear, which are very distressing and hard to control. People do not realize there is also a difference between anxiety and anxiety associated with PTSD. It is not about what might happen, it is what did happen....

My panic attacks however, tend to happen unexpectedly and very sudden. These are more severe than anxiety attacks and more intense, because these are sudden attacks of fear and losing control. It is not about five- minutes of feeling a little nervous. This is about a full-blown attack that I can go through every day. When I feel like I am going to suffocate and I need to find a way to get away. My heart starts racing and pounding through my chest and I struggle to take a breath. Then my body begins to sweat and my hands become clammy. Where I have a sense of dread and begin to fear the worst, because I then start to think that everyone can see that I am panicking and they all start looking at me which makes me feel a hundred times worse. The first time I had an attack I believed I was having a heart attack. It is the scariest thing ever. It is having constant thoughts rushing through my head, which I cannot control. Thoughts of things that may go wrong.

DEPRESSION

Disturbing Dreams

Everlasting Trauma

Panic of the unknown

Restlessness

Emotional

Suicidal Thoughts

Sleep Changes

Irritable

Overdosing

No Appetite

Depression for me, is a never-ending feeling of sadness and not wanting to do anything. In fact, there is no single thing that results in depression for me, rather several things, and here are just a few...

Disturbing Dreams. From night terrors to vivid nightmares, which are triggered by a variety of things that have happened in my life time that set off anxiety and panic, making me depressed.

Everlasting Trauma. Impacts on my thought process and feelings. Re-living my trauma every single day and night.

Panic of the Unknown. Intense feelings of distress and anxiety. Fear of places and situations, so prefer staying at home in case something bad happens to me.

Restlessness. Affects my mental state, in such a way that often I am unable to rest or concentrate, feeling on edge or irritable.

Emotional. I feel lots of feelings. Afraid, sad, lonely. I have trouble a lot of the time trying to express my feelings which include my sadness, and feeling hopeless.

Suicidal Thoughts. I have these thoughts a lot and sometimes they make me feel confused and scared and overwhelmed. I feel there is no point in living if I have to live this unbearable pain. I cannot imagine it ever ending, which is why I have attempted to end it all, many times.

Sleep Changes. Constantly awake, but when I do sleep, I have intrusive thoughts.

Irritable. I feel empty as though I have lost interest in everything, which then makes me sad. It has been a continuous condition, caused by my physical and mental health. The state I get in is an emotional state most of the time, which leads me to getting easily annoyed. Small things that would not usually bother me can make me feel agitated.

Overdosing. This is something I feel like doing a lot and have done a lot, especially when I am feeling so down, like there is no future for me. No point in living.

No Appetite. When depressed, I do not feel much like cooking, let alone eating. My stomach becomes knotted and stress and anxiety stops me from wanting any food. The feeling can become so bad that I start by missing breakfast, then lunch and before I know it, I've not eaten all day.

WHAT IS DEPRESSION?

(Trigger Warning: This letter contains mention of suicide)

My depression affects not just my mood, but my ability to think, to feel and to function. It shuts down all hope. I all too often wake up each morning not having the emotional strength to be able to face anyone. I feel like there is no pleasure or joy in my life anymore and it feels like my whole life is worthless. I have days where my brain is like a fog, as if it is all misted over and nothing is clear or positive or even makes any sense. Days where I do not know what I am doing from one day to the next and everything feels totally hopeless. Nights when I cry myself to sleep because of feeling so sad and nights where I just do not sleep at all because I have so much in my head. So, by the next day I am so exhausted that I have no energy. For me, it is a daily struggle in my everyday life. It is like having a trap fitted between myself and everything in my life. A trap that I just cannot get free from. Or being in a pool of water, that only I can see how dangerous it is. Having that sensation of drowning, like the water is filling up over my body and I am desperately trying to keep my head above it, struggling to breathe, and all I can do is hope that the day will never come that I will get sucked under for good and drown. It is seeing no hope, no way out, thinking my life is over. Sometimes I want my life to be over. All too often it has led to suicide. Depression is not just a couple of days of feeling low or sad. It is a serious mental health condition that can last for a very long time, even forever. It sadly takes many, many lives, every single year. Depression is not something you can just get over. It is a condition that should be taken seriously.

For me, it has been all my life. It is an illness, not something I can just snap out of. It is a fight. A continuous fight. So many people think that depression is all about 'Choice!' Why would I choose to be depressed? Why on earth would I want to face each morning with these dreadful thoughts in my head. Feeling such intense loneliness. Why on earth would I choose to be like that? To feel that every day? I do not have a choice. Depression is not a choice. It is an illness. It lives inside me. It controls me. Depression is a severe mental health condition and it can worsen very quickly and make other conditions I am struggling with a lot worse. It is not something I can simply 'snap out of' and people that have never suffered with depression would not understand this.

WHY SHOULD I HAVE TO HIDE?

Why should I have to hide my mental health disorders?

Is it because I am ashamed of being different from everyone else?

You do not understand, because you refuse to understand them.

So, it is easier to keep them hidden from you and pretend that I am
okay.

But I should be able to be open, to share how I feel

and for others to get that I too have feelings,

and when I have days of feeling totally broken

and I am sitting in a corner, crying my eyes out

I should not feel ashamed, I should be able to let someone in. Just
once.

But instead, I suffer in silence

because you choose not to understand,

because you do not know what to say.

It is easier for you to say nothing,

and easier for you to just walk away…

But it leaves me feeling more alone than I already do.

Imagine living in this world of staying silent,

when all you really want is someone to listen.

Well, this is my world.

So why should I have to hide?

WHY HIDE?

Why should I have to hide how I am feeling? But I do, because I am too ashamed to be open, which is why for so many years I have never got the help I have needed. I have never realized that I am damaging myself further both mentally and physically, by not giving myself the chance to feel and express how I am feeling inside, for so long. I have dealt with it, by keeping it a secret. By shutting it away. It is my traumatic problem and I have to try to find a way to cope with it. But I also hide it because no one understands, or more like no one wants to understand it. I hide my mental health a lot of the time, because that way I feel as though I can be 'normal,' rather than have people telling me that I am making a big deal out of nothing! So, it is better for me to fake it. Choosing to hide my mental health disorders also means I do not come across as weak to others, because sadly, that is what a lot of people see it as. Plus, if I was to disclose all that is wrong with me, I believe that it will not be acknowledged anyway. I hear the voices saying 'get over it' because they just do not get it. I try so hard to hide my physical disorders to, even though I am in so much pain. But I do not want to have people feeling sorry for me. A lot of my disabilities are hidden because they are what is called non-visible. These include my mental health conditions, my anxiety, depression, PTSD, chronic pain from my osteoarthritis and prolapsed discs. My glaucoma. My memory loss. These conditions are painful and exhausting and many do not recognize or acknowledge the challenges I face each day.

Why do I keep hiding? Because there is so much stigma against mental health disorders especially- I could count the number of times on one hand that I have been told that my disorders are just a cry for help! It is support I need and if I am not going to get that from the ones, I believe I should be able to rely on, then say 'NOTHING.'

 Just because I look okay, because I look good from the outside. Noone knows what is going on behind my mask! No one sees the pain that I am hiding.

LIVING WITH MY PHYSICAL HEALTH DISORDERS

It does not matter what you see.

Only you do not feel what I feel.

I may be in chronic pain,

but I try so hard to get through each day.

My body inactive, my joints stiff,

the sharp tingling- more than often numb.

So much pain when I move.

Just as much when I am still.

But oh… I attempt to keep going.

Depression kicks in and I feel as though the sheer pain will never go away.

The disability lives within my physical world.

This is me. This will always be me.

It does not matter what you see!

Because I know what I feel every day as I try so hard to hide my disorders-

Every moment of my life that I try so hard to piece together

attempting to take one day at a time.

Tired of carrying this heavy weight,

exhausted from hiding the real ME....

The me that is in a turmoil of pain.

MY PHYSICAL HEALTH DISORDERS

My physical health disorders are a combination of conditions that I have not only lived with for years, but some more recent. Chronic conditions that cause me so many problems every day. I have a variety of musculoskeletal disorders, including osteoarthritis which affect my joints, causing alot of pain and difficulty in moving about. Unfortunately, it cannot be cured. I also have prolapsed discs in my spine and in my c3 disc which affects the moving, bending, and rotating in my back and neck. The discs often press on a nerve root which causes a tremendous amount of discomfort along with weakness, numbness, and tingling, and can come on suddenly, most of the time, severe. I have had 14 operations including rotator cuff tear repairs on my shoulders, and been left with a considerable number of ongoing problems and tendonitis. I have had iridotomy laser surgery in both my eyes after being diagnosed with glaucoma and then in November 2022 I had a stroke. This sadly left me partially sighted, a weak left arm and hand and a very little short- term memory. My stroke has changed my life both physically and mentally and I now experience many feelings of irritability, forgetfulness, and confusion and no one understands because I am unable to control my mood and emotions. I live with my physical disorders every day which is not easy because they affect so much in my life, causing me acute stress and depression, along with psychological distress which puts an impact on my quality of life. My conditions are chronic conditions which affect my every -day living, including very low self-esteem and frustration, especially when I am in so much pain, but I have to live with this…. I am not saying all this for attention. I am saying it because this is how I must live my life along with my mental health disorders, but I also know that I am not the only one that suffers, which is why we all need to understand one and other so much more and be there for one and other…

I have to make out that I am not breaking inside from all the pain I feel. That I am not suffering, when really, I have this chilling numbness throughout my bones that I continuously carry as I ride these waves of hell, as darkness drowns my haunting screams of sheer agony and not a soul hears me.

MY SHATTERED WORLD

If only you could open the window to my soul,

you would see the pain I carry.

All the confusion I hold deep within my weary body.

Oh, how I wish to be understood,

for I seek desperately to be accepted.

Some days it feels like my world

is caving in on my fragile heart

and other days, it's like I don't

even have one.

Oh, how I wish

someone could recognize

this whirlwind that

I am drowning in.

To see the pieces of my damaged body.

These wretched days and sleepless nights,

as I attempt to survive in the darkest

corners of my shattered world.

MENTAL EXHAUSTION

My world has been shattered for quite some time now, which probably explains why I feel so mentally exhausted. Guess it's not surprising with all that I have been through and still going through. Even though I try to tell myself I mustn't fall apart and I attempt to keep going, but it seems the harder I try, the more exhausted my fragile body becomes and all I want to do is give up; for I am on the edge, tucked away in the corner of my mind, as tears well up in my eyes. It is hard enough coping with physical exhaustion, but mental exhaustion is a whole lot worse because my brain goes into overdrive and drains me and this crushing pain takes over. I feel as though I will never overcome the challenges that life has thrown at me and continues to throw at me and no one knows how I am truly feeling. The exhaustion that keeps burning through my skin. I am on the edge now, at the point of breaking and no matter how many times I get back up, life keeps pushing me back down again. My condition consists of extreme exhaustion and feeling detached every single day, making my life so daunting.

I am mentally drained from pretending that I am okay when I am not, trying so hard to keep everything together, when really, I just want to collapse in a heap and be done with it all, instead of keep fooling people. I know that when you read this, you are going to be wondering why I keep being so hard on myself all the time!

It is because I keep trying so hard and collecting pieces of my broken mind along the way, but then a huge weight comes down and crushes me to the ground and here I am, giving up again. I believe that I am a failure because no matter how much I attempt to fight through all this, I never win....

I wish I could explain the pain that burns through my skin and how each day it becomes so heavy, that I don't know how much longer I can tolerate it. The suffering inside, that bleeds away at my fragile bones, as I am left hanging from the threads of life.

Is it not surprising I keep giving up!

A PART OF ME

A part of me …

Is trapped inside this broken shell.

My mixture of emotions so want to escape

from this living hell.

Yet it all keeps pulling me down and suffocating my soul.

Overwhelming me with the darkest thoughts in which I have no control.

A part of me…

That is so overwhelmed,

I am unable to manage my very own tears.

I feel them filling up inside and I fight to

hold them back as I try to face my fears.

I cannot help but continue to live in the past,

where the demon takes over my life, takes full control,

for I believe it will forever last.

A part of me …

Lives in sadness, pain, and fear,

what is and what will forever be.

This is my life from now on.

It will always be a 'part of me.'

IT IS LIKE THIS

(Trigger Warning: This letter contains mention of rape and wanting to give up)

A part of me feels so trapped in this life I live, paralyzed by the fear that 'demon' has put me through. He took everything away from me and I don't know who I am anymore. I lost who I was, the night he brutally raped me. He took away the person I was. He has taken away my quality of life. I know I am not the only one that has been through and still going through so much and it is not easy; I can tell you that much. But I have lost control of 'me,' lost control of my emotions. I am not able to move on in my life because I am trapped in my memories, which make me feel hopeless, alone, and even scared of myself as well as everyone else. The world is a totally different place where I am at. A very dark place. I do not know if the way I feel each day will ever get better for me. All I know is I don't particularly like myself right now and the 'demon' has a lot to answer for. The impact he has had on my life and still having is unbearable. I never thought I could ever hate anyone like I hate him. Because of him, he has sapped the life from me. Taken away my confidence, my self-esteem, my trust, my wanting to keep living. I am stuck and I realize that it is because I am suffering and I have been for all these years, because of what that 'demon' has done to me. I have tried to hold on, in hope that things would change, but my life has just continued to slip through my fingers, leaving me more damaged within the darkness of my broken soul.

He is the one that has made me withdraw myself from so many things in life, from places to people. He is the one that has made me feel like I don't belong, the one that makes my life so gloomy. I want a life with a radiant sky and gentle breezes amongst sweet smelling flowers and feeling safe wherever I go. I have tried so hard, but it feels like life for me will never be okay again and that my suffering will never end. I will cling on, in hope that I can keep living, but I am not afraid to die...

It would be so easy to just give up- Wouldn't it?

I AM

I am…

The woman crying in the night

for the safety I have never known,

as I try to push the evilness away from the

nightmares that still tear the shreds of my sleep.

I am …

The woman hidden deep in the corners

of fear as I attempt to hang

on to the fragments of my life.

A sorry state of mind, composed of tortured

thoughts and fear engulfing me, as I cry alone.

I am…

Every bit of pain that fills every inch of my body.

I do not live my life to be pitied,

nor do I live it, to be judged.

Trust me…

I do not like being this way

But this is who 'I am.'

YOU DO NOT KNOW ANYTHING ABOUT ME

(Trigger Warning: This letter contains mention of suicide and abuse)

I feel as though I should be the only person that knows about my life. Because why would anyone else want to know about it? Who cares about what I have been through or going through? The fear and the sadness. The grief, the memories, the loneliness. The depression and anxiety, the PTSD, the demon, the darkness. My pain both mentally and physically. My everyday living, my feeling lost. My brokenness, my troubled mind, my suicide. My life... You do not know anything about me. You do not know how I am feeling or what I am thinking, neither do you know how much I struggle or how many times I cry myself to sleep at night. How many times I have screamed. How I have fought every day to not be the person I am. You do not know how much I have tried to forget the vicious rape that demon put me through. How much I have tried to block it out, yet still he destroys my life day and night with the horrific memories of him sexually, physically, mentally, psychologically, emotionally, verbally, and abusively destroying me. He has broken the person I once was. You do not know how many times I wish I was dead and how many times I have attempted to end my life. It hurts to be me. It hurts so much; you have no idea. I am not looking for pity, nor am I looking for someone to say 'Oh poor you' as I know I am not the only one that is going through such an ordeal. I know that there are a lot of people like me, that have had their fair share of pain and sadness and have had a far worse life than I have and there are others that just would not understand. But here I am, wanting 'someone' to know me for me and for what I am feeling. To know the full story of what I have been through and still going through. There have been times when I have so wanted to share how I feel with someone, but I guess I did not know what to say or where to start! But here I am now, sharing my life with all of you that are reading this. I was dubious at first, I must admit. As to whether I should pour all my life out to you, yet here I am not even half way through my book and you are getting to hear about my whole life. Going from no one knowing anything about me to the whole world that could possibly read this!

I do not want pity neither do I want to be judged. I just want to be understood. Liked for who I am not what I am.

SAVE ME

I have been hurt

I have been used

I have been broken

I have been destroyed.

I have cried tears of pain

I have cried tears of desperation.

I have lived in darkness.

I am lost

I am exhausted,

I am alone.

I am at the very bottom of my peak,

caught up in this web of no escape.

I lie hidden from the world,

for it is the only way I feel safe.

I hold on. Just keep holding on.

Waiting…

Waiting……

For someone to come

and save me.

CAN I BE SAVED?

(Trigger Warning: This letter contains mention of rape and suicide)

Will I ever know what it feels like to not wake up half a dozen times in the middle of the night in fear! Crying because I am so scared. Will I ever know what it feels like, to be free from the torture that races through my mind! Will the day ever come, that the battles I hold, will finally leave and I can once again live! Or will my life be caught up in a web of everlasting darkness, disappointments, loneliness, sadness, broken heart, pain, desperation, and exhaustion. Many a time I hide myself away in my own little cocoon where it seems to feel a lot safer than being out in that huge world of fighting all these things. It has taken me many years before I realized I have needed professional help. In fact, it took me until I attempted to take my own life, before I admitted something was wrong and it was not for the first time either.

I am probably not the only one that knows what it feels like to be struggling and wanting to give up. To feel absolutely crippled and trapped. I know all too well, as this is me, daily. Yes, life is so hard and so many times I think it can't get any worse, but it does. Some people say life is like a roller coaster and I get that because my life goes round and round all the time, only nothing ever comes to an end! I know the saying goes 'nothing is permanent' but it is being able to move on from what is troubling us, isn't it?

I know how destroyed I am and that all my pieces that once held me together, have shattered into tiny fragments and gone from what was

130

once a solid frame. Where I once stood tall, but now I am crumpled from all that has destroyed me. All the hurting that keeps on trampling through my bones. My emotions building and building up and I want to desperately scream out. How much more can I cry? I don't know if my broken body can take anymore. But because I am not open enough about how I am feeling or what I am thinking, everyone thinks I am okay!!

How can I be saved now? I am broken. I have been destroyed and I am caught up in this web of no escape. I am lost. I am alone. I am burnt out...

I believe this will always be with me, which is why I keep asking myself 'how can I be saved?'

IT HURTS

It hurts…

That I cannot just be the person I want to be.

That I am not enough as I am.

These fragmented pieces that have continued to destroy my life,

have left me broken in a world of turmoil.

It hurts…

To be this person… Alone.

Hidden behind the pain of my fake smile,

as I continue to wander, lost…

Searching and longing to be free.

Overcome by emotion as the cracks in my heart continue to break.

Barely keeping it together... Barely hanging on...

It hurts...

Cascading through the lost cloud of hope,

as raindrops fall like tears on my skin.

Surrounding myself in darkness, within the depths of my mind.

Along hidden paths, through silent streams.

I stare into empty spaces as my soul weeps

in every tear that falls from my eyes...

FEELS LIKE FOREVER

It feels like forever that I have had to hold on to so much in my life that it is hard to imagine ever feeling better. It feels like I have been fighting for survival for such a long time. I have longed to be free from the heartache and pain, the darkness, the fear, the tears, but it feels that my life has been so dark for so long, that it will never change. I often find myself asking 'What is wrong with me?' Overwhelmed with hurt, that at times I cannot find a way to connect with anything! Life for me, is so difficult that it feels like my heart is being ripped out and I just cannot function because my whole body gives up. For much of my life, I have held things to myself, thinking I was strong enough to do so, until suddenly I have had to let go. The trouble is, when things are so bad, I just do not know the best way of dealing with them. However painful, however much I want it to stop. It just doesn't. I guess I have hung on to hope for too long, believing it will all just blow away, like clouds passing in a winters sky.

I come across as a calm, happy person, shining bright-when really, I am broken, with tears in my eyes and a constant sadness that fills my heart. I have never wanted pity, just understanding. At the times when I am losing all hope, I need someone to show me how to move forward, from all that keeps eating away at me. I feel like I am stuck and I keep giving up…

How do I tell someone what is going on in my mind when I can barely get my head around it all myself? I do not even know who I am? But I know I am not enough, because I feel a failure and no one understands that. I don't want to hear 'you are doing so well; you have come such a long way. You are strong and such a positive person' No, I am not. People just think I am because I put on a false front. It is how I deal with my life.

Where really the colour has been taken from my world I once lived in so, so many years ago. Now, I live in a dark storm like a lost cloud, as I weep beneath the wild sky and my soul wanders through life, tired of carrying this heavy weight. I don't know who I am anymore! Day after day, I start all over again. Yet, the black clouds keep on hanging over me. I want to believe that one day the skies will be bright and my world will fill with colour again. I will keep fighting; I will keep waiting.

It is all I can do.

SORRY

I am sorry…

I am not who you want me to be,

but I try so hard to be a better person.

But in your eyes, I keep on failing.

I am sorry…

That I do not apologize for the things that are not my fault,

even when you seem to think they are.

That I am so broken, so damaged,

even when I try to hold myself together.

That I do not laugh, when you think I should.

But I do not have a lot to laugh about.

I am sorry…

That I do not walk around with a huge smile on my face.

Have you any idea how hard it is to fake a smile?

This is who I am. This is what my life is.

I am sorry…

If it is not who you want me to be.

I AM SORRY

Having mental health disorders is very difficult to speak out about, so all too often I must put on an act. I think a lot of people want me to be more than who I am. I cannot help the way I feel. Probably because most of my life I have tried to be someone else. I have tried to block out the bad things that have happened to me, which has been impossible most of the time. I feel almost as if I should be saying 'yes, I have mental health disorders' but I do not, because I am worried about what other people would think of me. There are things I am not sorry for; I am NOT sorry for my illnesses, for I have no control over them. But I am sorry for hiding them for so long, for keeping everything that I have been through, a secret. I am sorry, that I have never admitted I need help.

I have so many walls built up around me and have never known how to say what I feel. I couldn't explain why- But now I know it is a 'protection barrier.' After being hurt so much in my life, it is the only way I can keep myself safe. I have to live like I am in a prison, so no one can enter, only those that I fully trust. I am sorry, that I am so damaged, but this is who I am. Is it not surprising after what has happened to me! Here I am still carrying these dark memories in my head, suffering every single day and night, drowning in my thoughts, trying so hard to hold myself together. I often wonder how my heart keeps beating as it carries all this heaviness inside. All the pain it endures with every beat it makes. I keep fighting through every twisted memory that lives in me. There are no more whole pieces, for they have fallen, they have broken and the darkness has taken over and suffocated my soul. What life I had, was ripped apart a long time ago and I have lived ever since, trapped within my silent life of fear.

I try so hard to keep battling through and I cannot explain how difficult it is for me to keep faking my smile, pretending that I am okay when really, I am broken, yet I keep going just to please everyone else. Not myself. It is never for myself. Yet, most will never know just how much I bury my pain inside or how much my storms are hidden behind my blackened eyes as I cry.

I am sorry I am like this…

MEANT TO BE

I have days where I am not able to get up in the morning.

Where it all seems too much of a struggle.

So, I stay in bed where I can hide away,

curl up into a little ball and stay in my own little bubble.

So many days where I feel so overwhelmed

and I just want to let the world pass by.

Here in my own little cocoon

where I bury myself under my covers and cry.

Not a breath stirs from my aching body

as I lie in darkness, broken,

as my thoughts weigh heavily on my soul.

Not a word is to be spoken.

But it is what I am all about

I guess that is just me.

Maybe this is how my life is now

It is how I am meant to be...

ISOLATION

(Trigger Warning: This letter contains mention of rape)

I believe my isolation began from when I was raped because I never told anyone about what happened and I have been so scared ever since, which is why I have hidden away all this time. I do not choose to bury myself inside my broken body, more so that I do not have to face the world, because I am unable to cope in the big open space of this life, for fear of the unknown, so I retreat into the dark hole that hides itself inside my shell.

Because I experience depression and low self-esteem, I become even more isolated, as I find it too difficult to interact. If I am to be honest, I prefer to be alone, that way I do not have to risk anything that could, in my eyes, make a situation worse. If I was to close my eyes and think of all the people who I believe really 'get me' there would probably be 'zero' but that does not matter because I am the one that chooses to say nothing. I choose to be silent...I do not want to impose on anyone. It is better for me to hide myself away from the world and cope with it by myself. Only because not a soul understands! Maybe it is because this is who I am!

Isolation is my way of coping, because I do not want to speak to anyone or see anyone. It is why I use an excuse to avoid things like making out I have other stuff to do. Although, I never state what. I think it is because I believe I am an 'outcast' as well, so it is easier to avoid situations and people. This is how I survive, for I am convinced, that the outside world is not safe, neither do I want to risk anything that I believe is going to make me feel a whole lot worse. I have said so many times of how I feel. Maybe, I have never said it loud enough for anyone to hear me! Or maybe, no one has listened!

Why do I feel so guilty for being the way I am? Perhaps I am right to say nothing. That way, I wouldn't burden others with my issues and I wouldn't have this wretched pain like a sharp knife pressing down on my broken skin. Twisting and turning inside, waiting to bleed out. Maybe, I do not deserve to be listened to! So, for now, I will just keep falling. Keep on breaking, as I cling on to the tiny droplets of my tears.

For nobody notices....

ME

Day after day I wait…

As the tears continue to roll down my cheeks.

The pain in my heart spreads to my bones

and I feel myself breaking.

I wait…

In the darkness in my mental state,

listening to the voices inside my head.

Waiting for someone to ask if I am okay.

But nothing.

I wait…

As I crumble and lose control.

Sad and lonely.

Fearing and suffering.

My mind a battleground.

But instead of making time

to understand my disorders,

you choose to ignore,

for you only see what you want to see.

You do not see the real 'ME'

EVERYDAY

What people see on the outside is not necessarily what is on the inside. If you see me smiling and maybe hear the odd laugh, you automatically assume that I am alright and so, you do not think to ask if I am okay, because to you, by the looks of what my face is telling you, you assume that I am fine. All too often I appear to be happy to others and smile as if I am okay. When in fact I am breaking inside, but no one has any idea how exhausted I am from pretending that I am alright and I do this because I feel that others would not understand. Sadly, the world cannot see the dark circles that shadow my eyes because all anyone sees is the bright smile across my face.

So many people are in denial. Their perception of me is only what their eyes can see, not what is happening every day, because they do not know what is happening, they do not know how much I am suffering. Living with my mental health disorders, I worry more about telling people in fear of them not understanding than me telling them what is wrong. Nobody knows the REAL me, or how many times I have sat and cried and I do not mean a few tears. I mean a loud uncontrollable cry. Nobody knows the thoughts that I have in my head or how bad they are. My fears, my pain, my grief. No one knows who the real me is!

People just do not get what it is like to feel trapped and in darkness yet trying so hard to appear strong. I fake a smile because it is easier than to explain that something is wrong. Although it does not make it any easier for me, because all I am doing is hiding. Guess I am still trying to work on how to deal with this life, let alone cope! It feels as though there are so many pieces of me locked together, wrong pieces, and I am trying so hard to find the right bits that really belong, that can keep me upright, keep me fighting, yet all that keeps happening, is each section of me breaks a little bit more throughout the day and night and then I crumble, not knowing if I will ever get back up...

No one knows me like I know myself. Everyone just assumes that I am okay, but honestly, there is a fire burning away inside of me and I really don't know if it will ever go out...

I may look as if everything is quite normal, but on the inside, there is a battle going on.

I AM STILL ME

I may be broken from the inside,

my empty heart ripped out.

My emotions have taken over

and my mind, a book of doubt.

I may be full of hopelessness,

heartache, and pain,

and this life that I live daily,

is a never -ending drain.

Just because my soul is concealed

and I hide behind my mask,

my darkness is my light

and every day for me is a task.

For every tear and every smile

accept me for who you see.

I know I may not be perfect

and things go wrong, occasionally.

Just understand I am who I am

please like me for who you see.

Because no matter what happens in my life,

I will still always be me.

JUST AS I AM

I know I am broken and my emotions take over my entire body and my life is full of darkness. I know I hide behind my mask, concealing every tear that I cry, but this is me. This is who I am. So please do not treat me differently. I am trying every single day to heal my heart and to let light into my soul even though my emotions continue to knock me back, time and time again. Please try to understand who I am and what my life is for me because believe me this is a lot harder for me having to live like this than what is for you to understand! I know, not many people know how to respond, but I am still the same me on the outside, I just have a lot going on in the inside. Because of my mental health disorders, I am constantly made to feel a lot worse by so many others out there. Treated with a negative stigma and misconceptions and constant negative abuse, because, from the outside I look completely normal. Mental health disorders are 'invisible' and I should not have to feel that I owe explanations for the way I am. Yes, I am 'unwell' but why should I be classed as 'weak' just because I need help? There have been so many times I have been made to feel as though my mental health disorders are my fault. I have nothing to be ashamed of. They are medical problems which need to be addressed.

When I was first diagnosed, I failed to believe I had mental health disorders, even though I have been fighting them for years. I could not except that something was wrong with me, even though I knew deep down something was. I failed to accept that it is a part of me and that it controls me- Feeling anxious, worried, depressed, worthless, unhappy with emotional outbursts. Feeling withdrawn from life itself. Feeling scared and lost. Not trusting anyone because I feel everyone is out to get me. Believing the world is a threat to just me. None of these are my fault. I never asked to be this way, yet I am made to feel as though I am to blame every single day. Yes, I appreciate being given a little space to find the right path to follow in which to find myself again. But I should not be made to feel as an 'outcast.' I should not be judged. No matter what I have, I am still me. I just wish to be accepted for the way I am, aftercall I am a human being...

Just like you.

FALLING

I am falling…

Alone, in the middle of the ocean

with the weight of the world tied to my ankles-

Pulling me down beneath the waves,

my lifeless body sinking to the bottom.

My mouth gasping for breath

in this sea of hurt and sadness,

as I struggle to keep my head above the water.

I am this lost soul- broken.

Hiding behind my blackened eyes

in a steamy cloud of desperation.

This intense feeling that envelops and

suffocates my fragile body, as I finally give in.

Into this terror of darkness.

Trapped in a whirlwind of everlasting

disappointment.

I am falling…

ALWAYS FALLING

(Trigger Warning: This letter contains mention of rape)

There is no feeling worse than that pit at the bottom of my stomach because I have hit rock bottom. Falling, every single day no matter what. Knowing the next day is going to be the same. It is a dark, dark place. Where all my feelings are rolled into one. Where my emotions, such as hopelessness, fear, pain, sadness, and brokenness just will not go away. It is like I am drowning. It is like nothing will ever get better and I just do not know how I can make things better. I begin to lose my self-confidence and doubt everything. Believing to be a failure. I lose my ability to enjoy things and my appetite suffers and my sleep becomes less and less, and then I have no energy. Trapped inside my head, stuck in my own thoughts. Desperately trying to find a way out. When things become so bad for me, my life fills with negativity and I cling to all the bad thoughts in my head because it is all I know. My mind tends to keep me in that bad place most of the time which is why I am always feeling like I am falling, even though I try so hard to get back up. I fall so deeply, that there is no way I can get myself out on my own. I am crying while I am writing this because I am replaying memories over and over in my head, wishing that all the bad things that have happened in my life, never happened. I wish I was never raped. I wish my partner had never passed away. I wish I had never had a stroke. I wish my dad was still here. I wish I never ended up with mental health disorders or physical health disorders. I wish I could be happy.

154

My mental health triggers so many things in my body, which puts me in an uncontrollable state, sometimes not even I can control. All I do know, is that I want to get out of feeling like it. The 'falling' as if there is no end to any of the ways in which I feel, which effects every part of my body repeatedly. Changing every day, in every moment. The 'falling' as in falling apart. Because, yes, it is a dark place where I am at, no matter how hard I try to hold things together, they seem to spiral out of control. Right now, my life is painful because I do not feel as if it is going anywhere! I understand it is all part of life and that life must take unexpected turns sometimes. I wish so much, that instead of falling.... I could just rise.

THIS IS ME

How can I stop feeling like this?

My emotions running high.

One minute feeling okay then out of nowhere…. I am not.

One minute happy, the next, feeling so sad

that I wish I was no longer here.

My anxiety strangles me until I am fighting to breathe.

My body numb-

Like nothing matters anymore.

One minute, everything must be so perfect and the next…

I am worthless and life is nothing.

Trapped in this engulfing loneliness,

feeling emotionally unstable.

One minute I want someone to be around me

and the next I am pushing them away.

Short tempered and irritable.

You have no idea what I am feeling,

where my world ends daily

only to start again the next…

This is me.

ALWAYS

I know a lot of people that read this will find it hard to understand that my disorders are what I have to cope with every single day and night. For those that have never had to go through anything like it before, I totally get why you are not able to see what my illnesses are all about. Let me tell you. Let me explain a little better to you as to what it is like for me…

My moods, change in an instant, including how I think and feel. This is because of my mental and physical disorders and they all affect my ability to function. I can burst into tears for no real reason and find most days an utter struggle. I worry all the time, isolating myself from other people, because I find it difficult to trust anyone and I believe that everyone either loves me or hates me, nothing in between. Sometimes I push myself too hard, to try and be someone that I'm not, but then it triggers off feelings of panic and anxiety, making my everyday life so difficult. Days of feeling totally burnt out, feeling as if the world is crumbling around me. I wish so much that I could just block out the darkness and for once, see some light. I feel like a failure, to myself mainly, because I have kept things quiet most of my life. My illnesses are not something that I can control. They are more about trying to manage them. Because I have been suffering for a lot of years now, there have been so many times I have sat on the edge of my bed with a box of pills as the tears have trickled down my face and many times, I have swallowed a whole load of them, not seeing any other way out, for it has been the only way to end my pain. Am I considered as a failure because I can't cope?

For so long I have kept quiet, for so many years. I want to be honest now, about myself. I don't want to hide away as if I have something to be ashamed of. I don't want to suffer in silence anymore. Pretending to be fine, when really, I am crumbling inside, exhausted from battling these disorders.

I am struggling to stay alive… Yet nobody knows.

I AM NOT OKAY ...

To say 'I am okay'

is easier than trying

to tell you how I really feel.

You think I am strong,

but you do not see the real me.

The overwhelming pain from the tears that run

down my sullen cheeks,

as I drown deep within the rivers of my soul.

Each day I face the memories

of the most traumatic times of my life.

The loneliness, the darkness

and the emptiness

fills my fragile body.

All I can say is….

'I am sorry.'

I need people to believe that I truly am.

But I just need you to know

That 'I am not okay.'

NOT OKAY …

(Trigger Warning: This letter contains mention of suicide)

I am not okay, mainly because of my life and what has happened to me. Do you know what it feels like to be in a dark place? Overwhelmed by the thought in your head? Where you feel so helpless and each day feels as though it gets darker and darker that you end up feeling so trapped in your head that there is just no escape. Where you just want to curl up in a ball in the quietness and hope that this feeling will go away. But it doesn't. I am not okay and I am not sorry for the times I have attempted to take my own life. I am not sorry that I have wanted to be gone from here. I am sorry though, that you had to find out that the person you thought was so strong, could do something so drastic…. It must have broken you as much as my life is breaking me and I am sorry. I wish so much that I was not feeling like this. But I am.

So many times, I have attempted to take my own life. I hurt so much and I just cannot see beyond the pain. I cannot imagine it ever ending. I feel as though there is no point in me living because it feels like nothing is ever going to ever be any different for me. All I do is cry behind my four walls, hiding my tears from everyone. It is as though I am stuck. Stuck in this life that no one knows anything about, but me, and I am struggling so much. I am not okay… It's as if my life will not give me a break because right now, I am completely alone in this dark journey. I am breaking into tiny pieces inside, although I never admit that something is wrong. Why should I tell anyone? Because I know that unless that someone has ever felt the same way, then they would have no idea on what I am experiencing and then I am judged. Why? Because, I am expected to snap out of what I am struggling with!

My mental health Disorders/Suicide, is not something I can just snap out of. It is an illness. Here I am, hanging on to hope, caught up in this deadly gravity as it rips out my heart and tears away my soul…

ALL I HAVE

I did not choose to feel this way.

This loneliness filled with pain

surrounded by darkness.

A sea of emotions,

as my body sinks every day in my never- ending sadness.

My heart, an empty space, lonely and lost.

Listen to my sorrowful tears,

as my thoughts weigh heavily on my soul.

I am hanging on to hope

as I continue to walk

through these storms.

Momentarily drowning in this

troubled mind.

Lost and alone,

hopeless and heartbroken.

I am all I have.

IS IT ALL I HAVE?

(Trigger Warning: This letter contains mention of rape)

Sometimes it is not about who you have in your life, however close to someone you are, like I am with my family. I have tried to cope alone for so many years, being too ashamed to share half of what I was and still going through with members of my family. They know some of the things about my mental health but nothing about the rape or what it has done to me, how it has left me. I lost so many friends because of the way I am. Those friends just could not understand me, or didn't want to even try and understand. They walked away. So, I have lived most of my life trying to deal with things by myself because I felt it was the easiest thing to do. But it catches up with you.

Sometimes in life I do feel lonely and my emotions can suddenly hit me hard. Although, I cannot cope with being surrounded by lots and lots of people and people that don't get me. Especially when I am trying to cope with my grief and the torture that goes on in my head. No one that has ever felt like this could ever truly understand. Abuse, can never be understood either, unless it happens to you. So, no one has any idea how it feels or what it has been like for me. I have never wanted to be open about anything to anyone, because how would anyone get it? Which is why I have tried to deal with this all by myself. I pretend to be okay around people even though I am suffering inside. The chaos in my head takes over as I try to hold myself together. I am tired of fighting every day, because all the feelings are pulling me down faster and harder. It is a battle in my head. I often wonder how my heart keeps battling with all the pain it takes.

Myself, is all I have, because I am the only one who knows what has gone on in my life and what is still happening. I can only talk to myself about everything because it is only 'me' that understands what I am feeling, and if I want to scream out to myself, I can. I am better off being away from people, because they don't know anything about me…

All I want is 'peace.' A long path of complete 'peace.'

ALL THAT I KNOW

I did not choose to become the person I am today.

I keep on walking down the dead- end roads,

hoping to find a way out…

A way forward.

But I get sucked back in.

Trapped in a whirlwind of pain and disappointment,

falling into a terror of everlasting darkness.

I keep on looking for another path

in hope one will choose me!

But all I see are empty spaces.

I am this lost wandering soul…

Struggling in my every day path.

I am not the person I want to be,

but I settle for who I have become,

because it is all I know.

DARK PLACE

A place in my head where I am trapped and feeling helpless. A place filled with negative agonizing thoughts, with unpleasant surroundings of darkness. I know it is not going to be easy to get out of and I do not like being the person that I am and however difficult that may be for others to understand, it is who I am. This is a disorder, a mental health disorder and believe me, I so wish I wasn't like this. So many days, I just want to give up, because I am in a place where I feel totally helpless and time has no value. Where I feel so broken, so lost. Where nobody understands yet I am not able to explain. This dark place that I am in makes me fear so much, but because my life is such a struggle, it is where I have to stay because I do not know any different!

It feels like nothing will ever change. I am lost in my constant negative thoughts, with no way of ever escaping. As if I am in a dark valley of despair, desperately trying to be free from within myself. It is so scary as I struggle to fight my way out of this life I live in. I fear my own thoughts; my own feelings, and I am fighting back my tears as I write this, because it is as though I am locked away in a dark tunnel in my head, complete blackness, as I struggle to take each breath. I have no control over my thoughts and feelings because they control me. I cry. I cry so much, because no one understands how I am trapped in this dark place inside my mind. How I fight each day to try and escape it. Instead, it takes over until I have no strength left in which to fight.

All I ever believe is that nothing good is ever going to happen. This is what depression, anxiety, PTSD, and flashbacks do to me. They are what keep me in this darkness! I wish I could believe that it will all leave and a little bit of light could appear. Where glistening sun rays could fill the sky and brighten my life. Instead, my head hangs under a cold and lonesome cloud.

I AM THE ONE

I am the one….

That has no friends.

For I hide away in my temple.

My safest place to be, so as not to get hurt.

Battling with everyday life,

yet still manages to smile.

I am the one….

Who has lost my spark, yet is expected to shine every day.

Who chooses to live alone,

for being alone I cannot get hurt.

I am the one …

Who fades into the back ground

afraid of saying how I really feel,

as I fight the battles that no one knows about.

Those that will never understand!

My broken soul –

Drowning with emotion

in this heartache of no return.

IS THIS WHO I AM?

(Trigger Warning: This letter contains mention of suicide)

I am always asking myself-

Where is the blue sky and bright sunshine that once filled my life.
Instead, it is dark, lonely, and painful. Not even any signs of shining
stars that once lit up my world. Just sad tears that shed from my once
twinkling eyes, trickle down my dry aged face as my skin sits
crumpled from years of not being able to breathe. I am the one.... In
this heartache of no return. Alone.

I am in my own little world, hidden away in this huge bubble. Why am
I like this? My soul is broken, yet no one knows how I feel, because I
don't wear a 'label,' so there is nothing to peel off, to explain why I
have so many cracks within my body. I just tuck them away, so not to
be seen. I don't talk about it, because I don't want to let on that I can't
cope. I wish so much, that when I look up above, that the sky could not
only hear what I say, but send me a sign. A flicker of light to
acknowledge it understands me, or a droplet of water to cool my
feelings, a ray of sunshine, to break my fear. Because I don't have the
ability to pick myself up. Not anymore.

I have wanted so many times to just drive off the edge of a cliff, to feel
all the knots and turns as my body is thrown into a turmoil, for all the
bad things to leave my soul, to be free from the weight of the world
that has suffocated me for so long. To fall freely in mid air as the wind

blows through my fragile bones and the stars shine down on my once living being. No more pain.

I try to be everything that so many people want me to be, but not who I really am. I cry so many tears and live so much pain, and even when the sun is shining and stars are twinkling, my world is still full of black clouds as they suffocate my restless soul.

But no matter what I have going on in my head, in my life, or how many tears I cry. I am still me. I still exist. There may be pieces broken.

But every piece is still me.

FRIEND

I am that friend that is always there when you

need a shoulder to cry on

or just a friendly face to open your heart to.

But where are you when I need a shoulder

or a kind face for me to look up to?

I am that friend that listens to your problems,

however big or small, that is right by your side,

during the worst times in your life.

But where are you when I need to share my problems

during the worst times in my life?

I am that friend that supports your life completely

and wants you to be the best you can be.

That takes on all your troubles, even when fighting my own.

But where are you to support me?

To help me fight my troubles?

I may have fallen… I may be broken…

Yet I will always be the best friend I can be.

I just wish I had you…

To be there for me.

WHERE IS THAT FRIEND?

I am that friend that will do anything for anyone, whatever their needs may be. I will always be there for them, whether they are having a bad day and they want to share something or need to have a good cry or whether they want to just hang out and have some girly time. No matter what. I always try to be the best friend I can be. But where are my friends? Where are they, when I am having a bad day, when I need to have a good cry. When I need to talk to someone. When I need some company. I will tell you where they are…. they all left as soon as they saw how I became. Since I have been suffering with my mental health disorders and been struggling with life in general, I have been suffering daily and it is so hard to cope. I know a lot of people cannot handle it, mainly because they do not know the right thing to say so they tend to just walk away and that is exactly what they have done to me. Walked away. When I tell that so called friend that I am having a difficult time, I really hope they would be there for me like I am for them. To know the right words to say and to tell me that they will always have my back! Sometimes all I need is just one friend. One friend that will understand me completely. A friend that I can trust when I share my thoughts with them. A friend that will not walk away when the going gets tough. But those friends that I had simply walked away in which case they are not real friends. They are the ones that judged me because of my mental health. They were the ones I counted on and expected to stay by my side. I feel like I am always the one that is there when someone needs help or just a listening ear and many

178

times, I get told how much they appreciate me for listening to their problems. But when is it my turn? Why do they keep their distance from me because of what I am going through? I get they may find it difficult to understand what I am going through, but why abandon me at my most difficult times when I really need them? I get people do not like trauma and do not understand how to deal with it but how do they think I feel? Alone. The ones I believed I could count on have avoided me for whatever reason. They are nowhere when I need them. If they are not going to be there for me during my most difficult time then I do not consider that person a true friend.

I do not need friends if this is how it is always going to be. I am fed up with being let down and hurt.

SOME DAYS

Some days…

Are harder than others.

Where I just cannot bear to leave my bed.

Where my eyes slowly open and yet my body refuses to move

and the bad things still fill my head.

I am drowning inside and no matter how much my body tells me to

move,

my brain is saying 'no' and so this is where I stay,

for I feel I have nothing to prove.

I am wrapped in my sadness that consumes me.

A hollow emptiness that I cannot fill.

My head cries into my pillow and I close my eyes, as my body remains
still.

But as my hand clutches at my heart and the muscles in my body twist

My world goes dark... I am broken...

And my eyes are clouds of mist.

Help me to escape this pain, dislodge these tears

in which I have no control.

Or let me drown in the darkness inside me

and let me rest my weary soul.

THERE ARE DAYS

(Trigger Warning: This letter contains mention of suicide)

I know no-one can say that life is easy because in real life it is so hard and like the poem says, 'some days' are harder than others. There are many a day where I am just not feeling it at all. Days where I just bury my head back under the covers and that is where I stay. Tired, drained, broken, sad, lost, alone, in pain. Some days weigh me down, then anxiety fills me with panic at the thought of facing the day ahead. It is not just about constant worry that something bad is going to happen. It is the physical, mental, and emotional pain I go through more than I ever thought I would have to, it is so hard. I really do not know how my life ahead is going to plan out. That is if I am even able to make it that long. I know I need to be open more, about how I am feeling and what I am thinking, but believe me it has not been that easy talking about my deepest, darkest secret, especially when I have kept it hidden for so long. The last 36 years have been the hardest years of my life and I am so worried that I will stay stuck feeling the way I do.

So many times, I just want to give up. Days I cry, whilst other days I just scream as I don't know any other way to deal with this. I am not coping and I am not afraid to say so anymore. It is out of my control and I am struggling to keep holding on. This is not how I want to be, but it is how I am. In a whirlwind of emotions, to be honest.

Days where I just want to lock myself away in my room, where just myself can be in my own fear, my own sadness. So, I can let out my tears, my screams, having no one see the real me that I keep hiding. Instead, break down in a sheltered corner and let my pain out. Let the whole 'me' break out of my imprisoned soul and then tomorrow, I will face another day of pretending, as I hold back my broken tears, my hidden fears.

Once again…

THIS IS MY LIFE

There will never be a sunshine

that brightens up my day.

Or a wave upon the sea

that washes my worries away.

For my life is full of darkness

and my path is one dead end.

I can never be enough to help myself

my life is all 'pretend.'

Quietly I whisper

in hope that someone hears.

To help take away all my pain,

my troubles and my fears.

Maybe this is who I am

Only I wish it was a dream

For I long to live a quiet life

but instead… I silently scream.

MY LIFE ALWAYS

(Trigger Warning: This letter contains mention of dying)

How can I manage to find inner peace when my world is stuck in despair? When it feels as though much of my life has been in darkness and the paths that I have walked, have forever been dead ends! I feel like I am stuck on a long road and I try so hard to keep going, but make no progress. Even if I attempt to take another turning, in hope it will take me to a fresh start, it just keeps going back to the same place. I wish so much that I could change the direction of the path I am on, to a better place, but it just doesn't happen. Maybe I am not strong enough to change it. I do try so much, but the reality is, I can't. I cannot believe in myself, anything, or anyone. My world is full of negativity and it is a dangerous place. Unless you suffer with mental health disorders, then you would not understand what this means.

It's like I don't belong- in fact, I don't know where I belong! Or where I am supposed to be going even. I don't want my life to just be about keeping on going each day for the sake of it, I want it to be about wanting to exist each day. Yes, I have my family and I love them to bits, but when I am feeling at my lowest, I believe in my head that I have no choice but to die- That I have no reason to have to survive and the only thing I can think of is 'I want to die'...

My life, in my mind, does not contain 'reasons' for living, because I just exist. There is no sunshine that brightens up my day, or birds singing to melt my heart or make me smile. Just me, tangled up in my emotions.

The world feels so huge, so scary. It is like I am standing at the bottom of a wall, looking up. So, wanting to climb to the top and jump, to be free. Yet, here I stand, at the bottom, as I lose myself amongst the ever-falling bricks that crumble one by one, crushing my fragile bones.

I am drowning, suffocating and there is no way out from it.

This is my Life....

DAYS

There are days I feel nothing

and other days, my heart feels

as though it wants to explode.

My eyes cry like they never want to stop

and the smile on my face, disappears.

There are days I feel so alone,

occupied by broken thoughts

as I stare into empty spaces.

Every day gets harder and harder,

then I feel sad. I feel hopeless.

Yet I try to keep going

even when I am feeling at my lowest,

when I cannot find a reason to exist.

Even when I feel so lost.

There are days I wonder

if there will ever be a way forward

or maybe this is just how I am supposed to be.

Maybe this is how my life is to be lived.

MY LIFE EVERYDAY

Each morning and every night, I take a few minutes to just lay on my bed and I try so hard to think of something positive, but there is nothing that comes to mind, except negative thoughts running through my head and then the tears come. Gentle at first, then the more I become upset, the heavier they fall. But all the crying I do, doesn't change a thing. Having mental and physical health disorders makes my life a lot more difficult to live. I have a lot of painful feelings of hopelessness and sadness and ongoing fear. A lot of the time, I see and hear things that no one else but me can see and hear. Trying to fight every single day in hope that the next day will be a little easier. But it is exhausting trying to fight my situations I am living with and it feels like I am up against a brick wall. Every day feels like a challenge. Trying to find ways in which to cope with my feelings of worthlessness, fatigue, loss of appetite, grieving, suicidal thoughts. My feelings of emptiness, especially when often my traumatic event continues to rear its ugly head.

Living with what I live with, has an impact on my life each day. I have feelings of being overwhelmed, unable to manage or cope and this is when my anxiety kicks in and my heart pounds and I fear the worst. It feels as though my life has no meaning. No direction. I feel hopeless and numb. A lack of purpose. I feel as though there will never be a way forward for me, or even a way out of feeling like this. I wonder how I keep going sometimes. Everyone has something going on in their lives, I know that, and some probably worse than mine. But it doesn't mean that I cannot share mine with all of you…

The distressing memories and thoughts that take over my life, trapping me inside my own body and mind. Making me feel angry, helpless, and lonely, yet there is nothing anyone can do. I have had so much pain and cried so many tears and I have found it impossible to talk about my mental health disorders and all that has happened to me. I know now, that I cannot just let go and I doubt I ever will.

This is my life every day….

WILL I EVER BE ME AGAIN?

Feels like I have spent my entire life broken.

I often wonder if I will ever be whole again.

Ever be 'me' again.

All the trauma I have lived with, over so many years.

The 'demon' that has destroyed me.

My heart crushed, for the loss of my loved ones.

The sudden Stroke that has changed my life.

Sometimes I do not even know how to make sense of it all,

as I lie, overwhelmed by the thoughts inside my head

whilst my heart bleeds.

How was I to know that it would be so, so hard!

Yet here I am, battered and crumpled

as I continue to walk through this storm.

Tired of carrying this weight,

shattering pieces of my soul.

Momentarily drowning in my troubled mind.

WILL I EVER BE WHOLE AGAIN?

(Trigger Warning: This letter contains mention of abuse)

Each day I try to push through with all that has happened and still happening to me. My body has this heaviness about it and it feels like every inch of my once whole frame, has gone and broken into tiny pieces. I know I am not the only one to feel like this and no matter how mentally, emotionally, and physically drained I am, I am sure there are many that are experiencing similar things as me! This is not about needing to be fixed but more of needing to heal. Because of my mental health and physical health disorders, I face a whirlwind of pain every single day and night and the process is never ending.

My journey has consisted of crying uncontrollably and heart wrenching pain and it still does, every single day and night. I know I am always so hard on myself which is probably why I feel so wiped out all the time and I try so hard to break free from all that keeps holding me back, but all that ever happens is I find myself up against dead end walls, plagued with fear that pins me down, suffocating my frail body.

I kind of begin to wonder if there is ever a way forward in life! After I was viciously and violently abused, I kept it buried. I believed by keeping it hidden, it would go away, but instead it has destroyed my life. I have so many conversations with myself of how I wish I wasn't this way. It is like I am walking on eggshells, waiting for them to crack and for me to fall. I wish I could be walking freely on gentle ground, wanting so much for myself to flee from the pain that I hold inside. I need to get out. Out of my broken shell.

I try to erase all that has happened to me and keeps happening, but without success. I know that I can't change the past, but instead somehow find a way to live for today. I so desperately want to stop feeling this way. I do. I cry at night, hoping so much that things could be different, because I don't want to suffer anymore. I don't want to live with this feeling, that my heart is being ripped out.

There is no time line, I know that, but sometimes I feel as though I will always be like this. I feel like I will never be 'whole again.'

NO PLACE FOR ME

I am not the person you think I am.

I may look the happy, smiley woman that you know me as.

But underneath… I am locked away in my bruised

and battered body, hanging on to hope.

I hide the real me.

My pain… My emotions.

This broken mess, jumbled up inside my head.

My mental battles that no-one knows about

or understands.

But my soul is so tired of fighting,

tired of trying…

And I try so hard…

Leave me to hang under this cold and lonesome cloud-

In darkness…

Stay in a world where everyone has a place…

But me.

NOT THE PLACE FOR ME

This is not the place for this broken woman. But what do I do? I am trying so hard to be the happy, smiley person you see but little do you know it is not the real me. I am just this broken mess trying so hard to live in this place I call 'life,' only my life is a complete, utter mess. I am so tired of fighting and trying to be a better me and tired of pretending because I do not want to let my guard down and have everyone think I am weak. But I am. I am weak. I am fragile. I am broken. I have been knocked down so many times, that I have no energy to get back up.

Why does this feel like a world where everyone has a place… but me?

I wonder how I keep going, because my life has no point, no matter how hard I try. The path in my mind is not clear, so I never know which way is the right way. I look around at the people that surround me and wonder why their lives seem to be so much better! But maybe their lives are not better. Maybe they to have a life that no one knows about or understands. I am not alone then? Self - doubt holds me back from becoming the person that I really want to be. I certainly have always believed that my path was always so different from everyone else's.

I don't want to keep pretending. Pretending that I am okay. Have you got any idea how sad I have been? I don't know anymore, what I am supposed to do to make this go away. I don't have the energy to keep fighting through. I am so, so tired. I wish all my negative feelings could go away so I could find a way to re-live my life. I feel damaged. Utterly broken into the smallest of pieces and no way of putting myself back together again. I don't belong in this world, where I struggle in my every day footsteps, as thoughts flood my beating heart. I would rather drown deep within the rivers of my soul.

WILL YOU?

On the days when I am at my lowest

and I am unable to see a way forward.

When my tears are streaming

down my subdued cheeks and my heart

is pounding out of my chest.

On the nights when I am sobbing into my pillow,

struggling to get my breath,

not able to sleep from the intrusive

thoughts that fill my head.

The moments that I sit alone

in darkness, scared of my own thoughts

of what I might do.

Will you be at the end of the phone

when I call?

Will you sit with me and dry my tears

and calm my broken heart?

Will you listen to me when I tell you

that I am not, okay?

Will you?

WILL YOU EVER LISTEN?

(Trigger Warning: This letter contains mention of suicide)

Before anyone starts on about why I must not end my life and ranting and raving as to why I should stay alive, please, if you have no idea what it is like to want so desperately to die, then say nothing. I have lived so many years now in a very dark place and it really is the worst place to be. It is so frightening and there have been so many times I have just wished that someone would understand my feelings. All too often I feel the need to want to break down in tears, to scream out and say I am not okay yet I hold back, and I hide how I truly feel because who is going to listen? Who is going to want me to burden them with my problems, my feelings, my memories? Who is going to understand?

I fight every single day and night to stay alive, but nobody knows that. I wish so much that I could believe that everything is going to be okay every time someone tells me that it is. I wish someone could take away all the bad things that are going through my head and the pain that I am feeling every second of the day and night. But no one can and no one listens. Well, they do, but they can't do anything about it, however hard they try to convince me that they can. I just get filled with empty promises.

I feel like I have been on this journey forever and yet it doesn't seem to be getting any easier and I am so alone in my thoughts. My body is breaking, my mind is scrambled and my heart is heavy from my everyday living, where the world crashes down on my exhausted frame, as I try so hard to hold myself together. I breathe slow breaths, believing that I would be so much better off if I didn't exist.

I cannot find a way to break free from the chains that hold my life in these dark and dangerous thoughts as I continue to fight my battles that no one will ever understand. Noone will ever know just how much I bury the pain I hold inside, whilst the world carries on outside.

NO IDEA

Do not tell me that you know me

when you have no idea how my life is.

You do not see the scars that are etched in my heart

from the pain that I hold inside.

You do not see the blemishes I hide from the tears that I cry each day.

Do not tell me that you know me

when you never even think to ask if I am okay!

You have no idea what is going on inside my dark world.

You do not see inside my heart,

You do not see the loneliness I hide.

You do not live inside my head.

Or see the fight I fight every day

in order to keep on living.

You do not see me at my worst

on the days where I have nothing left

inside of me to save.

Do not tell me that you know me…

You have no idea who I am.

YOU HAVE NO IDEA

(Trigger Warning: This letter contains mention of suicide)

You have no idea who I am or what I am feeling, because if you did, you would make more of an effort to try and understand me, try and help me…. It is so soul destroying when I am forever let down, especially when I hoped I could rely on you, even just a little bit. I have gone through so many traumatic times in my life and feel so alone and suffering both physically and mentally. Anxious and overwhelmed, low, and sad, but you do not see it, because you see right through me. You do not see what lies behind my fake smile, or what is going on in my dark world, because you never ask, so I just keep on pretending. I mask my symptoms. I hide behind my smile to convince you that I am okay, because why should I have to keep on spelling it out to you, what is wrong with me! You have no clue how much I struggle, or how weak I feel. How much I am hurting. How much I am fighting this every day. So much so, that I have the same suicidal thoughts repeatedly, and have so many times, followed through with ending my life. Ending my pain. Wishing so much for it all to stop. Wishing so much that you would have the slightest interest in how this is all making me feel. You have no idea what this is doing to me let alone how I feel when I so desperately want to end it all. It is so damn easy to pop a few pills into my mouth and swallow, without even thinking about it. Oh, you may think I am being selfish as you have told me so many times. But you have no idea what it is like to feel this way. Like there is no way out from what is eating away at me. No end to it.

You have no idea who I am or what I feel. You have no idea of this unbearable pain that lives in my bones, that I am unable to imagine ever ending. Or how many tears I cry, because of the overwhelming, negative thoughts I continuously have. You have no idea how hard it is to have held on to all this pain for so many years, unable to tell anyone in fear of being judged.

Do not tell me that you know me. Because you have no idea who I am…

BECAUSE OF YOU

(Trigger Warning: This poem contains mention of Suicide)

Do not tell me that I am not alone

when I am clutching onto my pillow

sobbing my heart out in the middle of the night.

Do not tell me that you will be here for me

when I call you in desperation

and you tell me that you are too tired or too busy.

Do not tell me that I can call you anytime,

when I ring your phone and you do not answer.

Do not tell me that you care….

When clearly you do not.

One day you may just regret all the things

that you did not do,

when I am no longer around.

Do not cry for me then or pretend that you cared,

because it may just be 'because of you'

I took my own life.

THAT ONE PERSON...

I want to start by saying that this person is someone that I was led to believe would always understand me, or at least try, seeing as they have known me long enough. I never imagined that they would pretend to understand, yet lie about it. This person would not even admit what they did was wrong and to be honest, it is the biggest deal.

Have you ever had that feeling where you are at the lowest you have ever been? The worst you have ever felt, and you are so desperate to talk to someone...a friend. The friend that always promises that they will be there for you, no matter what and yet when you really, really need them they shut you down on the spot. We rely on our friends for a lot of things and we like to think that includes being there for us when things are difficult. I believed that my friend always had my best interests at heart and I trusted them to be around when I really needed them. I truly believed they would have my back. I liked to hope that I can rely on them when I need them the most, but all too often it is not the way. I have lost count on the times my so -called friend has let me down. I ask myself, is it because they do not want to know what is wrong? Is it because they cannot cope with the situation? Or is because they are just full of broken promises?

I am starting to believe that the reason being is they cannot handle my mental health, but at the same time, they really do not want to know what is wrong! Believe me, I have tried so many times to tell them how I feel. But that one person who I thought would take the time to listen to me, clearly does not. So now, I have lost trust in them. I choose not to tell them anything but rather just say 'I am okay.' It is better than getting constantly let down.

The reason for me writing this, is because I am disappointed. Disappointed that they let me down. I needed help, but I never got it.

Please do not promise me that you will be here for me. Please do not make promises that you forever break. Or promise to do whatever it takes to help me... I do not want 'promises' neither do I want you feeling sorry for me. I want you to be a friend, a friend that is here for me because you want to be....

Try

Try…

Asking me what is wrong before you judge me.

Like, what happened in my life and why I feel the way I do,

before telling me how I should be.

Try…

Imagining living with the trauma

that I have had to suffer silently with all my life

before accusing me of attention seeking.

Try…

Caring enough to understand how I must be feeling,

having lived my life a secret.

Not even telling those closest to me.

Try…

And put yourself in my shoes

and imagine facing this all alone…

When you are lost in the dark, full of fear.

Without saying a word.

Try…

Just once… To ask me, 'am I okay?'

BE IN MY SHOES

It is not easy pretending to be strong when really, I feel like everything is falling apart. But I cannot dare show it. It is the hardest thing to do, having to pretend. What I really want to do…. Is scream. I have lived with mental health disorders for so many years and not once told anyone about the trauma or any of the other things in which I went through, or how I am still feeling now, not even those closest because I fear the worst. I guess I fear I will be judged or not have any response at all, as well as fearing that the 'demon' will come for me. I feel it is easier to hold things back and say nothing. Easier to stay quiet.

 Imagine being in those shoes and think for a second, how would you feel if you had to face something alone. If you were struggling with the most painful moments in your life, unable to be open. Imagine living with such trauma that only yourself knows about. So many times, I just wish that I could wear a label around my neck listing all that is wrong with me so that people would know. It is hard enough being me as it is. For so long, I have pretended to be okay when I am honestly crumbling away and many a time, people tend to just stare at me without saying a thing, which makes me feel uncomfortable, instead of just asking outright with a simple 'How are you?' All too often, people judge me by how I am or react but, because I am on edge and have fears, I tend to react more so if someone just stares at me because it makes me feel unsettled. I pretend things don't bother me because I don't want to ruin how someone else may be feeling and I don't want to take away what happiness they may be feeling by burdening them with my feelings and thoughts…

Having to pretend that my mental health disorders do not exist, makes the problem a whole lot worse. Feeling ashamed of how I am and feel makes it so hard, so challenging. Holding on to my own thoughts and emotions is exhausting and all too often I feel totally burnt out. I guess I must recognize that this illness is with me and even after all the years of keeping it hidden away, I am now letting everyone know the truth and maybe…. Just maybe. Someone may just start realizing what it is like…

'To be in my shoes'

DO YOU REMEMBER?

(Trigger Warning: This poem contains mention of suicidal thoughts)

Do you remember that time I said I needed help.

The time I cried over the phone to you

telling you I wanted to end my life

and you told me to stop being 'selfish.'

Do you remember the time I reached out to you

desperate for you to listen and you told me to 'get over it'

said I was 'only thinking of myself.'

You never stopped to think about how I was feeling,

you never wanted to listen to what I had to say,

you never took the time to understand how desperate I was.

Do you remember that night I begged you to be here for me.

I tried so hard to reach out to you, because I knew it was going to be that night

and yet still you refused to help me.

Do you remember when I told you what I had done

and that I was feeling tired… I was slowly drifting away.

You could have stopped this,

you could have saved me from taking those pills.

But you left it too late.

REMEMBER WHEN!

(Trigger Warning: This poem contains mention of suicidal thoughts)

I remember when I was so desperate that I turned to the one person that I thought would be there for me. The one person that I thought I could pour my heart out to. The time I wanted them to be here, when I told them I wanted to end my life. I remember I tried so desperately to reach out to them, desperate for them to hear me. But they told me I was being selfish and that just made me feel a whole lot worse. Why do people assume that by wanting to end your life means you are selfish!! It is not about being selfish, it is being so desperate, so in pain, that we cannot find another way out to stop our suffering. This person did not want to listen, they could not even spare the time to even try to understand my feelings or how deeply desperate I was.

I remember when I begged for their support, asking for them to be with me and listen to how I was feeling. I told them I did not want to be here anymore and that I needed help because I could not see a way through. I begged them so much to be here with me. I tried so hard to reach out. It was like they did not believe what I was trying to tell them. My time was running out and I knew it, but still they would not come. I told them I was slowly drifting away. I had taken the pills, one by one, wanting to end the pain I was in. The unbearable thoughts that continuously filled my head. But where were they?

I remember when… I cried down the phone to them, telling them how I could no longer carry on. I desperately reached out to them, but they said I was being 'selfish' and that I had never stopped to think about how it would affect anyone else. Of course, I did. But I needed to end my pain. I could not live this life.

If only they would have come sooner. If only they had listened, they could have saved me from taking the pills. If only they had taken the time to understand how desperate I was.

But they left it too late…

BROKEN ME

If it was your ability to make me feel a lot

less of myself than I already do –

Then you have succeeded.

You have destroyed all that I had left of myself.

You have trodden on my weary bones and

broken them to pieces.

Taken the last breath that was left in my body –

You have left me to fall

when all I wanted was for you to catch me.

Left me in the darkness

when I longed to see the light.

You left me alone

when I so desperately needed to be saved.

You have not just cracked me….

You have utterly broken me.

WHO ARE YOU?

Many a time, this person has said that I can rely on them to be able to pour my heart out about how I feel. Whether it be mentally or physically. But, when I have needed to, what has happened?

I thought you were the one that I could count on. That I could trust when things are bad for me. That you would listen and comfort me. I believed you would be the one that would save me when I feel I have no one else to share my feelings with. I had convinced myself that you would be there when I needed you.

To say that you would be there for me! Where are you? Because I have not seen anything of you. You think because I keep on going, keep living, that I am not suffering! Well, I am suffering. I am hurting so much, but somehow, I have to keep going. I do not want to and I doubt you will ever understand that-

Who are you?

To tell me to trust you, to make me believe I could talk to you about anything and everything. Yet, when things get tough you are not anywhere to be seen. Who are you? To tell me that you care, yet find it so easy to ignore me rather than take the time to understand me. Who are you? To make me feel a lot less of myself than I already do. The times I have been so desperately grounded to the point of feeling lost in myself and hopeless and useless and wanting to give up. You have no idea how much more broken you have made me feel when all I was doing was crying out for help. Instead, you chose to ignore me. Because oh, it is so easy to do just that. You are supposed to be there for me like you keep telling me you are…But because of you, you have broken every piece that I had left inside of me.

I believe now, that you are not the sort of person that I should be having as a friend. I should not keep believing the things that you tell me. I should not keep believing that you are always going to be around for me. I should not build my hopes up, neither should I trust you.

A good friend would be here to support me and to listen to me 'Not to break me.'

LOVING MYSELF

How can I possibly love myself

When I cannot even 'like' myself....

Just a broken mess, with a mind like a meteor, waiting to go off.

Tears full of sadness, a heart full of pain-

Crushed with unbearable grief.

How can I love myself?

When I am a lost soul among the ever- falling leaves.

Shedding my skin that weighs heavily on my broken body,

as I fight these battles that live inside my head.

The trauma of the Demon that forever

destroys my inner being.

How can I love myself?

When I continue to wander in the memories

of my damaged mind.

Where I wish for a kaleidoscope of colour,

but instead, have a life full of 'Darkness.'

How can I love myself?

When my life does not feel worth living.

HOW DO I LOVE ME?

For all the things that have happened in my lifetime, I have come to realize that I am just not able to love myself because I feel I have let myself down. I should have been stronger and spoken to someone about how I have been feeling and maybe if I had got help sooner, then I would not have got to this point in my life, where I feel a failure…

Being emotionally, physically, and mentally abused is not something I can just get over. Plus, I do not have the confidence to face my challenges head on. It is not something I deserved, neither was it something I asked for. I am told, I should let go of my past. But sorry. It is not that easy to just let go. Neither is it easy to just shift my mindset. The whole thing is a difficult process, especially when I always think negatively. I constantly think negatively of myself and not able to accept myself for the person that I am. Most likely because of all that I have been through. The challenging life events I have been through. How do I love me? How do I even accept me for me? If I cannot, then how can I expect anyone else to! Somehow, I have lost my way. Fallen off the tracks of the pathway I was originally on. Because of all that has happened, I have fallen into a trap that I just cannot get out of. All too often I am putting others before myself and loving those around me, but not myself. Maybe, because I feel so 'broken.' All I hear are the voices of doubt, judging me. But this is how my life is and no matter how much I cry; it's not going to make things any better. All that has happened, is still here in my head and I have to live with it. I often wonder if I will ever feel anything positive again. Is there such a thing as a 'positive' path? Because I feel as though I have forever been on a negative one. I wish I could bring back the 'me' that I once was. The person that was so fearless. Truth is, I am not that person anymore. That part of me was taken, stolen and it has been tough ever since, to live this life that I live, carrying the memories, the scars, the heavy tears, and the broken pieces that once made me whole. Where is the 'me?' The person I was. The person I loved…. Instead, I am suffocating as I try to be someone that I am not.

In my eyes, having to love myself after my trauma especially, is having to begin again…

HELP ME

Help me to find myself...

For I am lost where I am.

My aching heart, my broken soul.

The darkness that engulfs me longs to be set free.

Help me to find myself...

To free my lonely, exhausted body.

To wash away the racing thoughts inside my weary head.

To dry my tears that flow from my sad eyes.

Help me to find myself…

Where I can smile again instead of cry.

For my heart to be fixed and my soul to be enlightened.

Where the light can engulf me

as it fills my body with hope.

Help me to find myself…

For I cannot do it alone.

HELP ME TO FIND MYSELF

(Trigger Warning: This letter contains mention of Rape)

I feel that being able to find myself is impossible. I am trying to figure out who I am and where I need to be, but all too often, I am not sure of my purpose in life. I feel as though I am just drifting along each day with no idea where I am going or who I am supposed to be...

Who am I? The real me? My true self? It is almost as if I am living in a shadow of who I once was, but come to a halt, not being able to move forward! My motivation has gone and life feels meaningless. It is like I am just 'here,' but I do not know why! It is as though I have no purpose, because my way of thinking is a blank and I just cannot see a point to it all. I feel alone because no one understands how I am feeling about myself or my life- There is so much going on that I feel I have no time to be able to even find the real me. Whoever the real me is?

I feel like I am being pulled in a hundred different directions as I fight my way through the suffocation that drowns me, having no idea where I am going! I try so hard to follow the right path, in hope that I will find myself again, but all I do is question myself on my troubled journey of continuous challenges.

My mind keeps on racing because it wants answers. I want answers. I have lost myself and all I feel is hopeless. So much has happened that I cannot even begin to believe that I will ever find myself again. I feel as though I am just drifting along helplessly, with no outcome and the longer this goes on for me, the more lost in myself I become.

When I look in the mirror, it is like I am looking at a stranger. I think I have spent so much time almost invisible, that maybe I have lost sight of who I am. Lost my way, my self-image and self-confidence. It is a struggle to even remember when I did not feel this way.

So many times, I just want to fall to pieces because I can't hold myself together anymore. I am fooling myself, believing I would ever understand all that I am going through. Some would say, I am lucky to be here and I guess in some ways I am. The night of the rape I could have died. So, I guess I can consider myself lucky that I am still here. However, it doesn't change how I feel. I still have to live.

Somehow keep surviving.

ANOTHER DAY

Another day....

Yet still I fight to hide this pain

inside my weary self.

Like part of my soul has died!

As I sit alone,

alone in my broken little world

in darkness.

I want to cry....I want to die. Alone....

Another day…

I keep falling, in hope that I will

get back up and try again.

This path of rockiness that keeps on convincing me

that I have no-one.

Maybe I am broken…

Unfixable even!

Another day…

I wear this mask to hide my pain.

Holding on to this torn and bleeding heart.

Suffocating in my silence.

ANOTHER DAY OF BEING ME

Another day of being me, in my broken little world…

People just do not understand what it is all about. I try to hold myself together every second of every day, when I tell everyone 'I am fine' when I am not, because people just do not know what to say. I hate it when people say 'pull yourself together' or 'get over it' or 'toughen up.' Do you think I enjoy feeling like I do? I am fighting this nightmare every single day and night. I cannot just snap out of it. If only it were that easy. Sometimes I do not even understand it myself. But this is my life, this is who I am. This is a huge part of my life and whether I want to believe it or not… THIS IS ME.

All too often I wonder how I keep going! It feels like my life is going nowhere and no matter how hard I seem to try; I just keep ending up back in the same place and find myself starting all over again. I try so hard to break free from my battles. But as fast as I can reach another day, they just keep throwing themselves back at me.

I feel as though I have been this way all my life. Constantly breaking, bit by bit, like a piece of glass. There are days I just want nothing more than to just fade away. I am done with struggling. Done with trying to be strong. Tired of pretending. Broken from living this fake life where I want so much to break down and cry. But all I do is keep pretending so no one knows any different.

I have fooled myself, believing I have been doing okay all these years, when in fact I have been breaking bit by bit. I never believed I would get to this, but now I have, I feel as though I am sinking deeper and deeper. Struggling to believe there will ever be a way out.

How do I keep fighting this? How do I keep fighting this Demon that keeps on destroying my mind, my life?

Every day is the same. Nothing ever changes. It is like I just exist!

LONELINESS

I hide myself away so no-one can see

the sadness in my eyes.

For no-one will ever understand

how withered and broken I feel.

Each day I struggle and suffer,

tired of this feeling.

Torn inside, when all I want is for

someone to open the window to my soul.

I am not asking to be saved

I am just asking for someone to listen.

To try and understand me.

To make sense of the broken soul that I am.

It hurts so much that I cannot be

what everyone wants me to be.

I am sorry that I am not enough,

maybe I will never be enough.

But I am not going to apologize for being 'myself'

when it is all I know how to be.

WHAT IS LONELINESS FOR ME?

For me, it is where I am feeling empty and alone. However, I do choose to be on my own most of the time because I find it easier to cope being in my own little bubble. Because I have kept everything hidden for so many years, I guess no-one would ever imagine that I was lonely within my own thoughts and feelings. Loneliness makes me feel lost and helpless, distressed, and anxious. Not being understood by others makes it a whole lot worse. Loneliness for me, is for many different reasons, including different changes in my life. I can be alone yet not actually feeling lonely, or I can have contact with people yet still experience feelings of isolation.

There are times when more often than other times, that I can feel lonely, especially if there are different changes that happen in my life. I know when my partner passed away and my dad, I felt completely lonely, yet I never showed it to anyone. I just sat in a corner and cried my eyes out. I felt that no one would understand the impact it had on me. My partner was the one I spent so much time with. We shared everything, and for him to pass away suddenly, destroyed me and then my dad. That was very sudden and a massive shock to, that I felt totally on my own. It was not until I no- longer had them here that I realized just how lonely I was and still am, and just how much it really hurts without them. When I had my stroke, the loneliness I felt then was a different kind of loneliness. My life changed totally. I had to somehow come to terms with the after effects. Something no one could ever understand. Even after the stroke, the rehabilitation and recovery were quite lonely.

But the one thing that loneliness is for me, that I love to have, is the silence. No loud noises. No loud voices constantly screaming in my ears. Just silence, and if I want to say something about what I am feeling, I can say it without anyone judging me with their voice talking over me. Plus, I can isolate myself in my own little cocoon. There are other times I so wish for someone to be with me. To take me into the light, remove my broken soul from the darkness that I forever live in.

THAT SMILE

That smile you see.

You think that is real!

I hide behind my smile-

It is really all pain and hurt,

but I refuse to give anything away so

I pretend that I am okay but really, I am crying inside......

When the sun rises in the morning

and I am wanting to stay where I am.

Then each night I go to bed and I tell myself

I will have a better night.

But it does not happen.

Instead, unable to sleep and at 3 in the morning

when I am sat in the quiet moments,

my head buried in my hands,

tears spilling down my cheeks.

My body is breaking all over again.

You have no idea!!!

That smile you see….

It is not real.

PRETEND SMILE

You think I am okay… but hey that is just me is it not! I put on this full frontage of smiles and chit chat to give you the impression I am okay… But underneath this so- called thick skin of mine, ohhhhhhhhh I am a complete mess. I am holding back every emotion you can possibly think of and it is not until I am completely alone that the crashing crescendo explodes inside of me. That smile you see…. It is not real.

I put on a fake smile to cover up what I really feel because I do not necessarily want to share my pain with others.   For example, grieving for the ones that have slipped away into another world has caused me to live with this pain every single day and no matter how much I think of the good times I had with them it does not make it any easier for me. Loss brings a deep loneliness into my life and I have become overwhelmed with the weight of the pain and heartache that I feel. Losing the ones I love, has changed my life, because of their absence, my future looks bleak and I have become very lonely without them and although I hold on to their love and take it into each day that I live, I know I will always have that big hole that they themselves once filled. I will never heal. I will never stop missing them and my heart will never stop breaking.

My pretend smile, hides the pain of my mental and physical disorders. I look happy to everyone else, when really, I am spiralling in a world of hurt that nobody sees. It is like I am constantly at war with the negative thoughts in my head and there is a constant feeling that no one gets me, no one understands what I am going through. Yet still I keep smiling. My pretend smile that no one knows about. Even if I am feeling empty inside. Low, sad, unhappy, anxious and anything else. I frequently hide how I am truly feeling behind my pretend smile. It is called my 'happy face' but nobody ever realises. I want so many times for people to know that my smile is pretend but I have just not been able to find the right words to tell them. But I realize now that I am just 'drowning' in my pretence-

DO YOU REALLY KNOW ME?

When you see me,

you see sparkling eyes and a kind nature

because you do not know what lies

behind my glowing smile.

You do not see the struggle I face with everyday life.

You do not know my journey of heartache and pain.

You do not see the brokenness behind my scars-

Instead, you see a strong, willed woman.

Proud and happy!

I long for you to acknowledge my pain,

to know the real me.

To realize how weary I am

from wearing this mask.

To know how broken I am inside.

Every single minute I am fighting a silent battle,

trying to survive another day-

So please…do not judge me by my appearance.

I am so much more than the eye can see!

YOU DO NOT KNOW ME

This right here….

These smiling eyes, this happy, strong woman you see! Do not be fooled. 'It is so easy to pretend' is what you are thinking. But 'NO' it really is not. It is so, so hard. You have no idea how tired and drained I am from wearing this mask and putting on this happy smile. Pretending that I am okay, when I just want to break down and sob my heart out and scream 'ACTUALLY, I AM NOT.'

All too often people look at me and tend to think that the person they see is okay, because they see a smiling face, only they do not see the cracks behind my smile. They do not see the pain that I am carrying, or the broken heart that has scarred my body. They do not see the fear I hide, the anxiety and depression. Maybe it is because of just that. I hide myself away. Not just myself, but all my issues to. My feelings, my secrets. My failures and challenges. I guess I hide all this because I am convinced no one would understand. I do not want to be judged or rejected. I do not have the courage to tell people who the real 'me' is, but I guess many will get to know who I really am, by reading this book.

It saddens me to say, that no one knows anything about me. I am a prison of mixed-up emotions, so many that are locked away and not a single person seems to be able to help me free them. All the dark thoughts that are inside my head. Instead, I will keep wearing this mask, that has become embedded in my skin, for I have become an expert on wearing it. People around me have never realized that something may truly be wrong, because I have never let on to anyone. It just seemed easier to not say anything…Why? Maybe it is because I have always had a fear that if others saw me for all that I have been through, that they would not accept me. But I am tired of faking. Faking my smile, faking my laugh. Faking that I am okay. I don't want this. I want people to know that this is not my real life, it is a fake and it is making me so miserable. I just want to scream out 'this is not the real me.' I am so exhausted with pretending. I am drowning in this pretence.

So please, do not judge me by my looks, because you really do not know what I hide underneath.

You really do not know the real me.

LISTEN

Listen to my silent whispers.

Listen to my tears.

To the sighs and to my screams…

Hidden within my broken body are the scattered

pieces of my soul.

Listen to my heart racing.

Listen to my breath as I panic in the night,

drowning in despair,

buried within my cold world.

Listen to the words I say to you.

Know that I am desperate for your help

and watch the tears as they fall from my eyes

as they try to tell you I am not okay.

Listen to me… PLEASE.

Listen to the message I am trying so hard to get across.

My message… so desperately waiting to be heard.

Listen…

PLEASE LISTEN

(Trigger Warning: This letter contains mention of suicide)

Well, here I am sharing my book about my darkest secrets. By now, you would have read some of the traumatic things that have happened to me. Things that I have never told anyone about and I am so grateful to you for getting to this point in my book and still reading it. Many times, all I have really wanted is for someone to understand how I am feeling. But not just me, anyone that has gone through or still going through hard times. We want to be heard…

It has not been easy to be open and express my true emotions. I have not actually ever told anyone what is wrong. Not even my family, because avoidance comes more easily to me than having to share such awful things that I believe would break them. Yet here I am now…Wanting to be heard. Wanting to be listened to for the first time in my life. Both my family and so many others, are going to find out the truth…. Right here in this book! I do not expect someone to fix things for me, but just to listen. You do not have to talk or do anything. Just hear me. Just read my words…

I have been through some difficult times, especially since what happened to me, and have even got to the point where I have become so desperate that I have attempted to end my life, several times. There is no easy way of just coming out with what I need to say because so many years have gone by after what happened to me and yet those memories are still etched in my mind. Still sit in my brain and they pop up every day and break me all over again. I have suffered with my mental health disorders for so long now and things are so hard that I cannot help but feel hopeless, lonely, and sad, not holding much hope of ever getting better and for those that have never suffered, it is unlikely you will ever understand. It feels as though the dark skies have been hanging over my tortured soul for so long now, as black clouds lower themselves, almost touching my fragile frame and troubled mind. A fearful storm, bursts through the deep ends of my heavy heart every single second of the day, cutting deep within my gentle self, as I drown within my emotions. It is so hard to keep going, only no one sees this side of me. No one sees how painful and scary it is for me, living in this dark place, battling with my emotions. I just want to be listened to. 'I deserve to be heard. Don't I?'

YOU CANNOT SEE ME

You cannot see me as I clutch my bleeding heart.

You cannot see what is inside me or what I fear the most.

You cannot see the pain I hide

behind the smile on my face,

or the overwhelming shadows

in the corners of my mind.

You do not know what I am feeling

or how much I hurt.

You do not see the emptiness I carry

inside my shell and when I look up above

where darkening clouds surround me,

you do not see the tears that roll down my cheeks

or how my body is breaking inside

and my bones are worn to the ground.

You cannot see me…

Even though I am right here.

RIGHT HERE

I am right here, but people only see what is on the outside. Noone sees what is on the inside, but isn't that what everyone sees?

I am forever overlooked by what is hiding deep within me, like so many others are to. People fail to want to know the real me as if I do not matter, because if I look okay to them from the outside then that is okay- But it's not. What I have is 'invisible' so unless someone asks, then no one is to know. Unfortunately, the world does not think. Barely anyone would consider what is on the inside of a person, as they only see what they want to see and each of us as individuals cannot change that.

Myself, personally having mental health disorders, would not just assume someone is okay. I would ask them, because of my personal experiences, I care enough to want to know if they are okay! Nobody will ever see the effort I make to try and get through each day, so I understand what it must be like for someone else.

Living with what I have, I have built walls around me, because I believe no one will get me if I block them out and I hide myself in my bubble, fighting my own battles that no one understands and I shall not let anyone burst it. Right here, there is this voice in my head that whisper so many frightening challenges and there is no end in sight as the sound takes me down a dark tunnel that leads to nowhere. My life is a winding road full of fear, but I am right here, dealing with my disorders every single second of the day.

I cry so many tears even when the sun is shining, all I see are dark clouds. I get that so many people probably have it a lot worse than me, but it doesn't mean what I have is not important. We are all in this together and I, like many other, do not want to be just here, to just be seen on the outside. I want my inner self to be listened to and if that was to happen, someone may just be saving my life.

TAKE TIME

Take time…

To look beyond the smile that tells you I am okay.

For you do not know the loneliness I hide behind my mask

or how every day I lose my way.

To look into my eyes and read beyond what you think they tell you.

For you cannot see the sadness that I hide behind them.

You really do not have a clue.

Take time….

To look through the things that are hidden within the depths of my
soul,

my weaknesses that you are unable to notice that I am unable to
control.

For all you see…

Are the things that sit on the surface, the things, only you want to see.

Instead of taking your time to get to know the real me.

Take time…

Just give me a chance, I will always be true.

For I have a heart and feelings, underneath

I am just like you.

TAKE TIME TO GET TO KNOW ME

It is so hard for me to write this, along with most of my other letters, because I have avoided talking about 'me' for so many years. Me and all my difficult times I have had to live through both mentally and physically. Take time to see the real person that I am, for you do not know what I am hiding behind the mask that I wear, that is covering the hurt and the pain that I do not wish to show. Just because I hold a smile upon my face, it does not mean that everything is okay. You do not see how this mask has embedded into my skin and that I am trapped within it. Unable to escape, unable to be free. Lost in a world of darkness. I just want you to take the time to get to know the real me. The me that is masked…

Each day for me feels as though I am living in another world! A world of haze and fog, where nothing is clear at all. I hide my pain, my unhappiness, my fears, my sadness, my loneliness. I hide because I believe I am unworthy. Because I am scared that I will not be accepted for who I really am. But you do not realize how hard it is for me, to have to pretend to be someone and something that I am not.

I all too often wish that I had options, instead of keeping on walking down the same single path that leads to nowhere. I try so hard to move a little forward each day, but keep slipping back into the turmoil that continuously suffocates me. Why can't I be different? Why can't I be free from this ongoing, exhausting pain? How much longer do I have to live in this suffocating world, trying so hard to survive? My disastrous life of suffering with the heaviness that keeps pushing deep into my body. I wonder if I will ever survive the war that continues to fight my fragile bones! But you know something…

I should not have to be made to feel like this. I should not have to hide behind my mask because I am worried about what others think of me. I should be accepted for who I am and if that is not the case, then so be it.

Because the only person that needs to accept me, is 'myself.'

THIS WOMAN

This woman…

She does not know how much more she can take.

How much more pain she must tolerate

as she tries to gather what strength

she has left in her weary body.

She carries the world upon her shoulders

with the darkness that fills her soul.

Like a leafless tree, she stands silent.

Her pain not shown, but just felt inside,

as empty echoes silently beat inside her.

She wants nothing more than to be free

of her pain, her shattered heart.

To be free of her trauma that lives inside

her battered body.

This woman…

Is 'ME.'

I AM THIS WOMAN

(Trigger warning: This letter contains mention of suicide)

The first time I admitted I was struggling, was after I attempted to take my own life and not after the first time either. In fact, several more attempts after, was when I admitted I needed professional help, because up until then I had been holding on to all the things that had happened in my lifetime, things that I had kept secret. I thought I could cope with it, but I couldn't. No matter how much I kept on going over what had happened to me, I could not change the past and even now, I still know that what has happened in my life, I will never be able to change, because they have happened and they will always be with me.

I knew I was struggling, way back, but never believed I needed help! I never believed I would end up the person that I am now, with so many mental and physical problems that need professional help. I am still me, so I do not owe any explanations to anyone about the person I am, but I will admit that I do need help. I am this woman that is broken and crumbling away. I am this woman, drowning in waves of sadness and pain, that are crashing down on me, pulling me under and I struggle so much to reach the surface. Gasping for air. I hate the woman I am, but I am trying so hard to fix me, but there is just too much going on in my head. Too much that has happened in my life that I cannot control.

How have I even got here? How am I still alive? I know I don't want to be, because I am suffering so much, hanging on the edge, waiting to fall. Wanting so much to just let go in hope that no one catches me. I don't know anything anymore, so how can I expect anyone else to?

I am this woman living in darkness, in pain that I tolerate with as I drown in my sadness because I have no clue in how to cope.

Not just to live, but how to survive.

I AM ME

She is the woman who has so many scars

etched into her body, invisible to all who see her.

Shedding her skin that weighs heavily on her soul,

as she cries tears of pain like droplets of rain falling from a burnt sky.

Most will never know just how much

she buries the pain she holds inside.

The woman who is a 'no one'-

Her fragile body chipped away as her

weakened bones fight to keep her upright.

Her soul tired, buried in this darkness.

The woman, who puts a smile on her face

and becomes whoever she needs to be,

just so no one would feel sorry for her.

As thoughts rip out her heart and tear away her soul,

as she lies in darkness.

She is not who you think she is....

Maybe she never will be.

Because she will always be 'ME.'

THIS IS WHO I AM

Many people who know me, would probably describe me as a caring, friendly, happy, smiley, shining woman. Well of course that is who you see, because you do not see the real me, do you? The real me is etched with scars, heart bleeding and pain that is eating away at my insides. My fragile body slowly chipping away, eating at my weakened bones that are trying so hard to hold me together. My soul weak as it lives in darkness. I feel broken, lonely, and sad, hanging on by a thread with everything around me crumbling into tiny pieces as I slowly melt amongst the pain within myself. I have come to realize, that I am holding so many wounds that have cut deeply into my broken soul and because people do not know what I am going through, it makes it so much harder for me. I just want to be accepted and for people to get me for who I am. To acknowledge my thoughts and feelings and how much I struggle every day and that it hurts to not be appreciated for the person that I am. I get that people do not know what to say a lot of the time and don't know how to handle mental health, therefore it is easier not to ask because they do not know what to respond with. Unless someone has mental health disorders themselves, they really do not get it and that is fine because I really do get how difficult it must be to know what to say.

Rather than admit I am an emotional wreck and fearing for my life every single minute of the day and night. What I really want to say is 'I am feeling awful. I am struggling so much that I am broken. I have no strength to fight anymore because I am crumbling inside.' Noone understands these storms that keep my soul from moving on. It is why I don't chase dreams anymore, because they are no longer within me. So, instead, I hide under dark clouds as I lie silent in hope that days will become gentler on my now ragged body. I will keep crying my tears and the world will continue to be heavy and nobody will see the real me just by looking at me, because I will keep my feelings hidden underneath and unless someone asks me if I am okay, no-one would ever know. But, just remember, I am not the only one fighting broken battles....

I am still here. You are still all here. Isn't that what matters?

SOMETIMES

Sometimes…

I just want someone to hug me

and tell me everything is going to be alright.

For someone to look me in the eye and say 'yes' you are enough.

To know the pain I am in

and the struggles I am dealing with every single day.

Sometimes…

I just want to be noticed.

I just want someone to see the real 'me.'

The one that is hiding behind my smile

pretending every day that

I am okay.

All I ask,

is for my troubles to be recognised.

To understand this life

I have carried for so long.

Just sometimes…

JUST ONCE

(Trigger Warning: This letter contains mention of dying)

So many times, I feel unnoticed, unworthy. But then I think to myself, is it not surprising! Who is going to notice my mental health disorders? They are not visible. How is anyone going to notice that I am broken? That all my pieces are jumbled up, tucked away in the corners of my mind, in darkness. I think I fooled myself when I thought I could get through this because I thought I could be strong! But who was I fooling?

Sometimes I have these visions of old, derelict windows lying in this barren wilderness of darkness, but there is no sunshine beaming through the single pains of glass, neither is there a storm of showers or even droplets that dampen the thin layers that shield each frame. Instead, behind each window is a figure of me. My arms reaching out and my mouth wide open like it is screaming to be released. Each face is of the true meaning behind my sad life. Some with cracks, some with loose skin crumbling away and others with no face at all!! My life has cracks and breaks in amongst it but behind each face there is nothing but emptiness, a blank canvas…

I have never been one to say how much pain I am carrying inside or the trauma that is within my bones and only I see the storms that I feel within my heart and carry the memories that only I know about. Only I know my deepest secret that I keep locked within my soul. Noone sees how trapped I am, which is why all I think about is how I can set myself free! I suffer so much, but I have learnt through my struggles that I am not the only one to be feeling this way. I am not the only one that has mental health disorders and I know I should worry less about what others think of me and just focus on simply trying to find the best way to free myself from this life I have carried for so long and the only way…

Is to die.

IF EVER

If ever…

There is a time when you may just ask me if I am okay.

Instead of me saying 'yes.'

Instead of me holding back my tears

and putting on a fake smile.

I will break down in front of you

and let my tears run down my subdued face,

as I cry uncontrollably.

If ever…

There is that moment that I am not actually okay.

I hope that you will hug me and tell me

you are here for me.

I hope that you will listen to my pain

as I pour my heart out to you.

To understand me.

To care.

To hug me.

Just once…

THIS MOMENT

(Trigger Warning: This letter contains mention of dark thoughts)

I have so many moments of emptiness and feeling lost, like I just want to break down in tears and I so wish that someone could be here. Even if it just means handing me a tissue, or giving me a hug. It is what we all want isn't it? But sometimes, it just is not that easy, as I have learnt over the years. I am afraid to be open or even to burden others with my problems, because I do not know where to start, so I feel it is best to keep quiet a lot of the time.

I am not the strong person people seem to think I am. Quite the opposite in fact. I get upset at the slightest thing and being so fragile, I break easily. But no one sees this side of me, because I hide it. Perhaps it is because I am unable to let anyone in. Who is going to understand the storms that take over my body, the aches and pains that eat away at my bones, the sadness that takes over my distorted shell and the fear that eats away at my blackened eyes as the tears bleed from my fragile face, as I fade away in darkness, inside my mind. Noone will ever see me like this, for I hide it well.

I wonder how I keep on going each day and if I will ever find a place where I do not feel threatened. If I will ever be free from the fear that drinks its way through my veins, and ever rise from the grave in which my body is stuck in.

I believe I have this evilness that has been forced inside me and that my bones have ripped me to the core. That demon has destroyed my once delicate frame, which is now wittering away. There is nothing left except for my shell that lies on a cold, dark slab, my knees pulled tight against my chest, as I suffer in silence.

I have nothing left.

BUTTERFLY

Like a delicate Butterfly with broken wings,

I lie alone, silently processing the pain that I carry.

Nobody wants to even try to understand me,

as I lie, trapped within this solitary space,

dissolving into my whirlwind of thoughts,

as dark clouds hang over my head.

Singing eternal notes of sadness,

I wrap my body in layers of silk.

My heart, unable to ever dream of being whole again.

I ask myself... will I heal?

My wings torn and tattered,

no longer able to carry me.

Trapped within my memories,

my freedom denies.

And as I cry...

I wonder if my wings will ever be fixed,

if I will ever be able to fly again.

If I will ever be free!

OH...TO FLY AGAIN

I have lived so many days, so many weeks, so many years of carrying so much pain and here I am, still carrying it, impossible to let go. I am so tired, so drained from struggling with these loads that keep pushing me back further into darkness than what I am already in. I feel as though I am in an expanse of water, slowly drowning as I sink faster and faster. I want to find a way to be free from this, to be able to breathe again…

Oh, how I wish I was like a butterfly, to be able to see the world from a distance. Fly through the clouds taking in all the amazing sights and lapping up the sunshine and the breeze that gently blows through my wings. To soar above all the negativity that continues to eat its way through me and fill my body with love. How amazing would that be?

Oh…. To fly again, but instead I am trapped within this solitary space. Trapped in my own mind, a prisoner in my own thoughts. Desperately looking for a way out. Sometimes I go for days of being disconnected from the world around me, when all I want to do is break free from the life I am trapped in, but I am yet to evolve, to awaken from where I am, longing to develop into the next stage of my life. I guess my broken wings are holding too much pain to be able to carry me now.

I do not want to be the Butterfly with broken wings. I want to change, to grow and to transform. To live free from pain and sadness. To receive comfort and hope. To fly high and achieve happiness and positivity, and for all my prayers to be answered. How I want freedom, instead of being like a caterpillar, shut down in darkness in its cocoon. I want to explore like the Butterfly and be free in a new world. To relive.

I do not want to keep feeling low, to have no purpose. To have no strength to carry on. To constantly feel trapped. I want to fly without fearing anything bad is going to happen to me.

OH... IF I WERE TO FLY!

If I was to leave this life of mine,

to fade into the distance of yesterday.

If I was to have a choice of a different being.

I would choose to emerge as a 'Butterfly.'

To spread my wings in the open air,

releasing the pain that I hold inside,

letting go of the negative thoughts,

the crying in my heart,

the tears that softly glisten my dreams.

To learn how to glide,

to flow within the breeze,

as each flap, I take another breath...

As my wings unfold, I will soar into the sky

and fly...

Fly high

TO FLY FREE

Oh, how amazing would it be to be a Butterfly of delicate beauty…

To float upon a breeze. To flutter around a loved one, letting them know I am with them. To fly free and not have a care in the world. To be able to let go of all that pain that I have held on to for so many years and fly free from all that has lived in my head and destroyed me over time. Oh, to be free from the brokenness that I have held on to for so long. No longer would I be fragile nor my soul weak for I shall fly free in the wind and be the strongest I have ever been…How amazing would it be! If only it was possible to be able to fly like a Butterfly! But that is never going to happen, so instead, I guess I must try and 'fly free' from all that I am feeling. All the stress and pain. The grief and sadness. The trauma and flashbacks.

All easier said than done! There are many things I have been told by various professionals and all too often I find it almost impossible.

I am struggling, lost in this place that I don't belong. Unable to find the correct path. I want to fly. Fly free from this pain, for I have become weak and can no longer fight. My wings are so delicate right now, but if only I could fly into the open world and escape all the bad things as I swoop through the air free and at peace and enjoy every second of freedom.

Maybe one day my wings will open and I will be able to fly free….

MY STEP DAD

It takes a very special person to do what he did.

To love me and treat me as his own.

I count my blessings for all the special times we had

and I will treasure all the memories that we made.

I am so sad that he had to go,

but grateful that he is no longer suffering.

I never told him enough

just how proud I was to be his step daughter

and how grateful I was to him

for always finding the best in me,

even though I can never see it in myself.

For always giving me the best, he ever had.

I miss him terribly, but I know he keeps watch over me.

I thank him for being the most amazing step dad

that he did not have to be.

Yet he was the kindest and gentlest man that kept me going

with all the right words that he could ever say.

I know I can never bring him back,

but I know I will see him again.

So, for now…. He can rest in Heaven.

WILL ALWAYS REMEMBER

21st May 2003 R.I.P

The day my kind, funny and caring step dad passed away after several strokes, his body finally gave up. I remember it like it was only yesterday. Sitting by his bedside at the hospital with my mum. He had had another stroke and wasn't even awake. Just lie there in the bed, still. Not even the slightest of movement came from him. His once gentle, kind brain had shut down. It was just his heart keeping him alive and somehow, he just kept on fighting because that was the kind of man he was, never giving up. Keep fighting was what he always used to say to me and I always admired him for that. This once fully alert, chatty, smiling man that loved everyone and everything was lying here totally unaware what was happening to him and then sadly, he gave up. He stopped breathing. He had fought for so long to keep on going, but not for himself, for everyone else. Because that was the kind of man he was. Always putting others first.

When he died, I felt as though I had died to. I was in so much pain that my grief suffocated me and for a long time it was unbearable. He guided me in so many ways in life, and I miss that so much. But even though I no longer hear his voice, I still feel him close. I still feel him trying to guide me in his own little way.

I want to say a huge thankyou to him, for not only being the man that he was in treating me as his own, but also to thank him for being the special man that my mum needed in her life.

There are so many things I wish I had said to him, but never got to say. Mainly a huge 'Thank you' for being such an amazing step dad. I will always miss him and I will never forget him. Being a step dad, being my step dad, made him a very special man. He was one in a million and I will always be thankful for the kind, thoughtful and caring man he always was.

He would do anything for anyone and he did everything for me.

YELLOW ROSE

Sweet soul

her beauty conveyed such kind messages.

She bloomed out of the darkness

and blossomed into the light

carrying her warmth, her affection.

Her beautiful kind soul

weaved from threads of magic.

Her eyes glistened like pearls

and her words laced in gold.

Like the flower, she embraced the sun

as she lit up the world,

making the smallest of moments special.

The memories I have of her

are like petals of the 'rosebuds' I hold in my hands

and will be with me forever.

Even now, as 'broken' as I may feel

I will always remember her

as the beautiful 'yellow rose.'

LIKE A MUM TO ME

04th June 2018 R.I.P

From the very first time I met her; she welcomed me with open arms. Made me feel part of the family from day one. I believed she would be around forever but it was not to be, because after a long illness, she sadly passed away. My partners mum and like a mum to me. It broke my heart; it broke everyone's heart. I just could not believe that this beautiful lady was no longer going to be around, no longer be in my life. She was one of a kind, was Sue. With a beautiful, gentle heart. I will always be grateful for the time we had together, but I so wish she was still here.

I will always cherish the beautiful memories and all the love and support she gave me and always be thankful to her for offering guidance when I needed it. She was a very special lady, although would not take any nonsense, but if I needed her, she always made herself available to listen, like a mother with her daughter and she was always here for me as a friend to. She never judged and more than often, would wipe my tears away. There are so many more things I wish I had said to her and I wish so much that I could have the time back, to see her again, because it hurts so much to not have her around.

Like the poem says, she was a sweet soul that always blossomed in the light. She lit up the world. She will always be in my heart and I will always love and miss her immensely. I will always remember her as the beautiful 'yellow rose'

Rest in peace lovely lady.

BROKEN HEART

Some things can never be replaced once lost…

The words of a loved one

when the one you love has gone.

I have been trying to survive.

The spaces my loved one once filled are now empty.

It is so hard to accept that all I have are memories.

It is so hard trying to cope,

knowing my love is not coming back.

The hardest thing is having to pretend

that everything is fine, when really it is not.

There are moments when it seems like

time moves so slowly and it is like

he has only just parted from this world

and yet there are other times when it seems like

he has been gone from my life forever.

I do not think people will ever understand

the pain I go through.

Until it happens to them…

It breaks your heart.

HEARTBROKEN

04th April 2020 R.I.P

John was my partner. He meant everything to me. He had a stroke very suddenly and then got sepsis. On the day he sadly passed away, the world became a lot darker than what it already was, for me. I spent the whole day at the hospice with John, talking about how much we loved each other and all the things we were going to do once he was better, because I still believed he was coming home. He was so, so tired that day and in so much pain. I suggested he try and get some sleep and that I would stay at his side, but he would not sleep unless I left, so I promised him I would see him in the morning as I really wanted him to get some rest. He smiled and said he loved me and I told him I loved him to as I kissed his forehead. It was an hour later when I got the dreaded phone call to say he had passed away shortly after I had left his side. I honestly could not believe it! It was as if he knew, but he didn't want me to be there when it happened, even though I so wish I had stayed by his side. It left me broken and there are still moments now when I wonder how I possibly had any tears left to cry. My tears fell heavily down my face that evening and all night. In fact, my crying was uncontrollable that it physically broke me. It really was the worst pain to ever experience. I did not ever think that it would be, but it really was. One minute I was with him, enjoying his smiles and taking in his laughter. Talking about the memories that we both made together. Hearing the words 'I Love You.' Then suddenly…He was gone. It has taken my life.

We never got to say goodbye. He was never meant to leave. We were talking just a short while before, about all that we were looking forward to. He kept smiling. I think he knew it was his time, because he kept telling me that he will forever love me. When I left him to sleep, I did not think for one second that my heart was about to be broken, for my world to shatter. I still wish he were here and that I could have another day with him, another week, another year. It will always hurt. I will always be heartbroken. The pain has scarred me and it will live with me forever. I do not care what people say, but grief is forever and John will be to. He was not just my love, my soulmate, my best friend…. He still is.

MEMORIES

Here I stand, behind my perfect smile

as I hold back my tears.

that so want to fall from my eyes.

My heart bleeds, with every breath that is drawn.

Whilst a searing pain streams through my broken soul

from the weight of the world that I hold inside.

I fight, each day, to survive the turmoil I am in.

Unable to escape into the 'normal' that I so long for,

as I break down once again.

Drowning in the sea of sorrow,

memories flood my heart,

as I wander as this broken soul, into darkness.

Spiralled into a world of hurt,

I hold the memories, deep within…

Of my love that slipped away.

MEMORIES OF HIM

Memories are all I have…

Some days it feels like only yesterday and other days, it feels like a life time ago. I sit here thinking of the last time I saw him, the last time I heard his voice. Then just at that moment, every memory we ever made, comes to my mind, as tears stream down my cheeks and the image of his smiling face fills my head and my heart breaks all over again. His smile would light up a room. I felt everything with him. I will remember all that we made in our lives together, all the beautiful times that existed, because of him. He was my missing piece of my puzzle. He was my forever dream, my forever happy ending. I am broken without him. Losing him from my life has been one of the hardest things I have ever had to live with. I would give anything to have him back, even just for a day. I was never ready to say goodbye and I will never be able to except that he is gone from my life. Now all I have are the memories that we made…

And oh…. What memories we made. We had some real quality time together creating so many unforgettable moments, but I wish so much that we had taken a whole lot more photos. I have so many memories of him, of us, here in my heart in which I will hold on to forever.

To suddenly not have John with me anymore in person is the worst thing and I wonder how I have managed to make it without him. All too often I ask myself how I have got through each day. It is not easy. No matter how many times people tell me it will get easier, it just doesn't. It will always hurt. I will always miss him. I will always wish that I had more time with him. I think about all the things that I may have said or wished I had said. The things I had done or wished I had done. But instead, all I have are memories…

John will always be with me, for I will carry him with me, wherever I go.

WHAT I HAD

Sometimes, I ask myself how I make it through each day!

Everyone thinks I am strong and coping with life.

But the truth is- I am not.

I am struggling every single minute of every day,

with the pain in my heart from my grieving.

The everyday I must face picking up the pieces of my broken body.

Trying to mould them back together, to make me 'whole.'

But the cracks continue to appear as I break down again.

I just want someone to recognize

how much I am pretending to be okay... When underneath, I am
broken.

How every day, I put on a false smile and carry on as if all is normal.

But inside my weary body, I am crying out to be recognized

as my broken soul deteriorates...... minute by minute.

Wishing I was strong enough to carry my sadness, but instead,

it pulls me under, deeper into a dark hole...

Drowning in my emotion, overwhelmed by my loss.

Knowing what I had...

Will never come back.

WILL ALWAYS REMEMBER WHAT I HAD

I went back to the hospice on the evening of 4th April 2020 to say my goodbyes to John. He lay there looking so peaceful. No more pain, no more suffering. I kissed his forehead and held his hand and I told him 'I love him,' then broke down in tears. So, what if I broke down. Unless I did, I would just continue to keep holding it inside until the day would come that I would break. I am allowed to cry; I am allowed to feel hurt and none of that will ever go away. Love does not end just because I have lost the man I love. I never wanted to imagine a life without him because he was my world. My heart was broken that night and still is. I cannot pretend that everything is okay or will ever be okay. I will always remember what I had because he will always be around me, even though he is not with me in person, he is in my heart and therefore everywhere I go.

I am the usual me of pretending that I am okay now where I hide my feelings from the outside world, where I often wish for my heart to stop beating, if only to be with him again, as crazy as it sounds. It is not until you suddenly lose someone that you love so much that you realize just what you had and it hurts so, so much when you suddenly do not have them in your life anymore. Knowing that you cannot see them, nor hear their voice, nor be able to touch them. Nor have a future with them.

No matter what may happen later in life, it does not mean that I will forget John. The memory of him will always be a part of my life.

John's memory will always live on inside of me, no matter what and in everything we ever did. Every kiss we ever shared. Every smile he gave me. Every moment of love, every laugh, (I will never forget his laugh). Every minute of togetherness that we shared. I will always miss him. I will always miss him next to me. Wherever my life takes me, he will always be with me. He will always be remembered.

MY GRIEF

Some days it feels like I am not even here.

Days where I just feel numb and then the tears start....

The tears that scream from my soul

and once those cracks begin to split,

it is then that my heart breaks into a million pieces

and the pain suffocates my entire body.

This pure burning heartache

that eats away at my insides,

as I think about the last time he held me

in his arms.

My soul tired,

caught in this deadly gravity,

spiralling into this world of hurt,

barely holding on.

This is my pain…

This is my grief.

GRIEF PAIN

The day I got to see John again was at the chapel of rest. I knew it was going to be hard, but I just had to be with him. He lay there looking so peaceful, like he was just sleeping. I read my letter to him that I had written and for a moment I believed he was going to open his eyes! Tell me that it was all a bad dream! But as I continued to attempt to read the letter with tears streaming down my cheeks, I knew he was not going to open his eyes and that he was not coming back.

Losing John has been one of the most painful of pains to ever feel, to ever experience. It has absolutely broken me and missing him is like nothing I have ever missed in my entire life for it has ripped my heart out and I would not wish that upon anyone. I do not just miss him as a person. I miss the sound of his voice, his cuddles, his laugh. I miss going places with him. Even just watching a film together. Having a stroll at our favourite place we always used to walk together. The worst thing about losing him is the 'emptiness.' The not having him around anymore. That 'empty' ache of longing for him but knowing that he is never coming back. It is the most painful experience ever. I feel like I am in a massive bubble, suffocating, yet unable to find a way out. I cannot accept what has happened. I never will, because it should not have happened. There was so much more that should have been done for John, but sadly it was not. I am still angry. Why? You may be asking!! Because more should have been done for him. That much I know. That much I believe. I will never come to terms with

John passing away. I will never be able to accept what happened and I will never be the person I was. The pain of John passing away has made me realize that every tomorrow will never, ever be the same again. In fact, they will be unbearable and I will cry tears of sadness day after day, night after night, because my heart is still broken and it will be like it forever. I am hurt and I am totally exhausted. No matter what anyone says. Grief pain changes you because trying to get through each day is almost impossible. I will forever love and miss John and there will always be a hole in my heart that will never heal. I will keep on grieving for him. I will keep on crying and one thing I do believe, is knowing that John is with God now and I know he will be taking good care of him and with his beautiful mum too.

PICTURE OF MY GRIEF

I try to pretend that I am okay

inside my brokenness,

as I ache from the wave of grief

that washes over me.

A light went out in my life the day he left

and as I fight through the darkest of times,

searching for a way forward

and the ground beneath me becomes fragile.

I become engulfed in this raging storm inside

my head.

He is in my thought every morning

and last thing every night,

as I hold him in my heart…

I will carry him with me for the rest of my life

and when my time is done here,

his soul will whisper to me gently,

as I find my way home … to where he is waiting.

MY PICTURE OF GRIEF

There really are no words….

John is missing from my world now and I cannot describe how truly difficult it is to exist without him. The world keeps on moving and I am exhausted from pretending that all is okay, when it is not. I pretend to be fine and the next I can be on the floor almost holding myself as I rock backwards and forwards sobbing my heart out, that sometimes I think the whole neighbourhood can hear me. The truth is, unless I just let myself go, it will keep on building up and building up until I get to the point, I just cannot hold it any longer and believe me because I have done that.

How do I 'get over it?' Or am I supposed to somehow get through it?

Losing John was one of the most painful of pains. He was taken from me, without any warning. It has felt like a knife thrusting into my body, twisting, and turning and feeling as though my heart has been ripped out. It is brutal, it is devastating. It is like an endless ocean that continuously rises above my body, pulling me down and drowning me, day by day, and nothing, absolutely nothing, is strong enough to save me and take me back to water's edge, back to dry land. I know I will always hold on to all the time we had together and I don't have any answers in this letter, because my grief was thrown at me so suddenly. It is dark and very tragic and it has completely knocked me back and left me feeling so lonely. There is no normal, and the hardest thing about losing John, is that there is nothing I can do about it.

I wish so much I could bring him back, but I know that is not possible and the worst thing is waking up every day realizing he is not here and never will be again. For me, it is like a world of darkness.

There is never an ending to grief, not in my eyes anyway.

THIS IS MY GRIEF

I hide my pain that is eating away

at my weary body.

Even on my worst days

I manage to smile,

just as my tears still fall

as it consumes my life.

This pain that I live with cannot be seen,

for it is trapped inside my bones.

How do I tell you that I am so broken?

How do I cry

when I must pretend that I am okay!

Let me grieve in the way that I need to.

Let me do this in my own time.

However long it takes…

This is my Grief.

THIS WILL ALWAYS BE MY GRIEF

By writing this letter, it is not just about telling you of my sad loss of John, but to tell you how grief is for me and how it is possibly for a lot of others. I don't have any answers about grief, but I can tell you, that it is the worst thing to hit you, especially when it is suddenly. Grief is tragic, it is the most painful thing to ever go through. It certainly isn't something I can ever accept. The sadness of losing John will always be with me.

It is like someone is ripping my heart out. His absence has left me feeling empty and lost and deeply, deeply sad. My heart breaks repeatedly as my tears fall from my eyes. My sorrow breaks each tear like a shattered piece of glass against my already broken body, as each breath I attempt to take, tangles itself within my lungs. My grief eats away at my bones as it brutally rips me apart day by day, tragically taking bit by bit of what is left of my mangled self.

The day of Johns funeral was the day I was dreading. Seeing the coffin sat there, knowing I would no longer be able to see him, feel him or hear him. No longer feel his kisses, feel his tender touch, have him hold me in his arms and tell me he loves me. No longer hear him call me his princess. It was all so final…. This was the end. I feel as though I am on an emotional roller coaster and no one understands what I am going through. It feels like I am the only one that knows my pain.

I feel like since John has been gone, my life must to because I am lost without him. I really do not know what I am doing with my life and wish he could send me some guidance. Grief is very difficult to get my head around. The reality of it is very hard to imagine, until it happens to you. Trying to survive the loss of a loved one is the worst pain ever. Whether it has been 1 year or 3 years, it is still so very devastating. I still have not healed. I still have moments where I suddenly burst into tears. I still feel very sad. I am still living for the times that were, the times we had. Which is why I still feel 'Broken.' When he died, I died.

THIS IS MY LIFE NOW

The second I saw him

I loved him.

I knew he was the one for me.

From the first time we kissed,

he stole a piece of my heart.

The taste of him on my lips-

That took my breath away… and in that moment

I knew I could never be without him.

He set my imprisoned soul free,

but he left an imprint permanently on my heart.

It is just me now,

drowning in a world of emptiness,

as I lie enveloped by multiples of darkness

-Alone-

This is my life now.

ALONE IN MY LIFE

As the curtain slowly closed around him, I realized that I was never to see him again. I got outside and completely fell to bits. I broke down and cried. I cried so much. My heart broken into even more pieces than it already was and then it hit me…. This is my life now….

I wake up each morning and many times I wish that I was not here. I often wish that I could be in beautiful Heaven, then all this heartache and pain and struggle and nightmares, would all go away and I could be with my love again in a calm, quiet, peaceful place. I would not have to keep on fighting all the every-day thoughts in my head and the negativity that keeps on rotating in this brain of mine. I would not have to keep drowning in my world of darkness, keep trying to hold on to some hope of light. I am still hurting. I am still so sad. I am so, so lonely and most of the time I wish I was not here.

It is so hard to live alone after you lose someone you love. Another day without them, another day of missing them. I so regret that we took each other for granted. We took every day for granted because we thought we had forever. I never thought for one minute that it would come to this, that we would be without each other so soon. I have not only had to learn to live without him as my partner but also as my best friend, my soulmate. There are so many times I have needed one of his hugs, needed to see his smile. He had such a gorgeous smile and his laugh was so infectious. I never believed that I could ever be without him. It is so hard to carry on when I have been so used to having him in my life for so long. I suddenly feel so empty. I never imagined a world without him in it. It is strange, but whenever I go to the crematorium and have my chats with John, somehow, I do not feel as close to him as I do when I chat to him at home. Believing he is still here with me is all I have to hold on to.

I guess all I can keep telling myself is that I will not always be alone, I will see him again some -day.

It is not 'Goodbye' but 'See you later.'

SILENTLY

Silently…

In darkness, shrouded in mist, all is still.

All but the clock ticking in the distance.

Let me drown in the depths of my broken body

as I sink deeper into the unknown.

Lost in the mists of time like tangled dreams

wrapped up in my sombre thoughts.

Silently...

I sit, staring at the walls-

Not a sound to be heard except for the tears that drop

onto the blank page of my Journal.

I weep for my loss.

I dwell on the heartbreak of him missing from my life,

my head filled with a wistful of memories

as I live in my world of silence.

SILENTLY I SIT

In my own little world, I sit and think. How I miss him being here in my life, sharing the days of togetherness like we used to. Silently I sit, as tears roll down my cheeks, remembering all the things we did together, the places we went. The laughs we shared. The words he spoke, the smiles he gave me. His soft gentle kisses that made my heart melt. Our togetherness. Silently I sit…As I dwell on the heartbreak of him gone from my life, as I live in my empty world with nothing but memories. The world feels a dark place without him in it. I miss his voice, his laugh. I miss all the special moments we shared. All the hopes and dreams we had to look forward to. All the things we used to do, the places we went. A moment of silence is a time I quite often reflect on as to what has happened. All too often I sit on my own in silence and think about what was and how the life he and I once had has now stopped. Trying to process the fact that he is no longer here. Thinking about facing the rest of my life without him. No one will ever understand the pain that I feel until it happens to them. The waves of intense sadness and emptiness. Even loneliness. A whole roller coaster of feelings. Ups and downs. I feel like I am drowning in my sadness. But as I sit in silence, I remember the times that we had together. I am not okay, for my heart will always be broken from the loss of him and my life will never be the same again. No one will ever understand the pain I feel, or how alone I am without him. How much I miss him.

Since John passed away, I have felt that I need to deal with his loss by myself in silence. Simply because no one understands how I feel. Losing him so suddenly has made me live my life in a way that I have had no other choice but to live. Although, I have never felt so lonely, so lost or so unsure of myself or where my life is ever going. People are carrying on with their lives as normal but I can honestly say I have no idea what 'normal' is! But I know what pain is. This is pain. The worst pain ever and however much it hurts, no one else sees it. Losing John has been such a lonely journey of emotions that I always wonder how I carry on! I do not want to keep telling myself that he is not here anymore. I know he is not here in person and that breaks me, but I do feel his presence all the time and hold on to the thought of one day, seeing him again. No longer sitting in silence by myself....

HOW DO I?

How do I…

Love myself enough to stay when the one I love has gone-

I try to see the reasons in which I must carry on.

In hope, them alone will be good enough for me to keep on breathing.

How do I …

Stay above the waters of life, but instead sink deeper into the depths of despair.

Attempting to hold on to the faith that holds my pieces together.

To rest my fragile body, hold my pillow as I weep

and fill my empty heart with all the memories we made.

How do I…

Even begin to start over again

Lost in this turmoil of sadness.

Drowning inside from sorrow and heaviness that fills my heart.

How do I…

Love myself enough to stay….

When the one I love has gone-

HOW?

When John died, everything changed. It was like my whole life stopped. I miss him. I miss his smile and his laugh. I miss the life we had and what we had to look forward to, together. It is not fair that he had to go and no-one knows how bad that feels until it happens to them. I never thought that grieving could hurt so much or go on for so long. Having to continue with life without him is an endless sadness of unbearable pain. Grief is a process, I know that. But how do I possibly love myself enough to want to stay? I spend a lot of time trying to find answers as to how? Usually without any outcome because I always feel further away from the actual question. I do ask myself how would he feel if I just gave up! I know he would be saying right now that I must give myself time, but time does not seem to be changing anything. I sit here thinking about the last time I was with him, the last time I heard his voice and then tears roll down my cheeks and the sound of my crying is uncontrollable as I catch glimpses of his smile, knowing I will never see that smile again. Not in this life. How do I stay above the waters of life, when all I feel like is drowning? How do I stay when everything feels so raw still? I try so hard to live each day even with all that I have going on in my head, in my life. But truth be told, living my life without John here, is not the same. My life feels as though it has no purpose. I miss spending every day with him. How do I carry on without him?

This is my message to John. I may still be here, still living, still battling. Still facing my challenges. But my body is still fragile and my tears still fall and my heart is still full of all the memories that we made. All the places that we went, all the laughs that we had. But I am still lost in this turmoil of sadness for you. I am still broken. It still feels like only yesterday that you slipped away and I know I will never heal from the pain of losing you. I still walk through every memory that we made and still feel every ounce of love that you left in my heart. I sometimes wonder how I can possibly cry any more, how I can possibly love you more than I already do. I will keep on re living the moments we had and will keep on missing you. There is no guarantee that 'time' is going to make me better…But I guarantee I will see you again one day.

A LOVERS' DESPERATION

(Trigger Warning: This poem contains mention of suicide)

I lie silently in my room

as I swallow my last pill.

No sound but a gentle breeze

as my body now lay still.

I can no longer go on living

since my love has passed away.

For the pain that I am feeling

grows stronger by the day.

Locked in a life of yesterdays,

a world I can no longer face.

I want to be with my love again

no longer be here in this place.

Drowning in my emotions

as another day I try to find

where everything is so still and silent

and his last words imprinted in my mind.

DESPERATE TO BE WITH MY LOVE

(Trigger Warning: This letter contains mention of suicide)

I never believed that what happened would happen, especially seeing as he was so young still. I spent most of my time with him, and so to suddenly be without him, to not have him in my life anymore has absolutely broken me. I think each day about how I desperately want to be with him, where he is. I do not just 'want' to be with him. I 'need' to be with him. He is my everything. My love, my best friend. My soulmate. The one who always made me smile. The missing piece from my life. He was my world and to be without him is breaking me more and more each day. I never thought for one minute I would suddenly not have him in my life, because we were always together. I believed he would always be here with me.

I miss John because he was a huge part of my life. I find it almost impossible to carry on without him. More than often, I sit silently alone, drowning in my emotions as tears fall from my eyes, remembering all that we had, yet will no longer get back. Just thinking, just remembering, all the time in which we had together. I thought we had forever… All the memories we made will now only ever be memories. The last words he ever said to me and the last vision I ever had of him, will always be engraved in my heart, imprinted in my mind. It is so hard living without him in my life. Trying to survive every single second, minute, hour without him.

So many times, I have attempted to take my own life because I have wanted to be where he is, with him. Desperate to be in a world of love and peace and kindness. To stop feeling all the things I am feeling. To get away from this pain. This brokenness. This forever feeling of sadness. How do I go on? How does anyone go on when they have had to say goodbye to the one they love?

So many people say 'you're so strong. You're coping so well.' No, I am not. It looks to so many people that I am. That is because I have to make it look like I am. But really, I am falling apart.

John will always be a part of my life and I will always be desperate to see him again and until then, he will stay here in my memories I have of him. The memories that we made.

TOGETHER AGAIN

When there is no path in front of me

nor a simple direction in which to follow.

Stuck in this place I am at, this life full of hurt and sorrow.

There is an emptiness in my heart and soul

which will never be filled again.

How can I possibly move forward

when deep inside I am full of pain.

Feeling sadder as each new day begins,

never again will I ever shine.

As I search for a way forward,

attempting to live one day at a time.

He will forever be etched in my memory,

always in the 'what could have been.'

No words could ever be enough,

but my tears shall always be seen.

I will hold on to my love in my heart,

knowing one day we will be close once more.

We will be together again,

just as we were before.

TOGETHER ONCE MORE

Life for me is tough, what with my mental health and physical health disorders and no day ever seems to get any easier. It feels as though I have been dealt one knock back after the other and I know there are far worse off people than me, but because of my disorders, I sometimes struggle to see that. My head is bombarded with so many negative thoughts and feelings that I am just not able to shift them. When John died, I died. My whole world fell apart. The whole of my inside was crushed into tiny pieces and still is and my life was no longer my life and still isn't. Not being able to see him was and forever will be the most painful pain I have ever felt. A never ending, devastating time to ever go through. The most intense feeling of sadness ever. I felt then as I do now, that I have lost part of myself. I feel empty, like part of me is missing. When John died, it was like I had to adjust to a life by myself. Live in a world where he no longer existed in. It has been so hard, because he always existed in my life. I don't believe there will ever be any sun shining on me anymore, not without him by my side.

I long for the day that I will be with him again, in heaven. No more tears or pain. No more struggling with my every- day life. Side by side spending eternity together, growing closer and closer just like we once were here on earth. Until then. I will ache for him every minute of every day and night. Cry tears for him. Whisper sweet messages to him, but also keep him in my mind until my life here is through.

I am thankful that I have my belief in the afterlife, because if I did not, if all there is, is a few years of living and then leaving this life to nothing, then it would mean I would never see or be with John again. I am not here to live, then die and go nowhere and see none of my loved ones again. So, for now, I have to keep holding on…

Like a chain that has been broken, our links will join once more and we will be as one.

STROKE

There I was in a different place. My life changed.

My life had changed so many times but this was different.

It was like no other moment I have ever been through.

Here I was…dizzy, disorientated,

and feeling helpless.

My left side had been affected and my eyes unable to focus.

My sight was gone!

Oh…How scared I was.

Taken to hospital by ambulance, left for 7 hours in waiting room,

being told it was just a migraine!

Eventually a CT scan, then the news I dreaded.

A stroke....

The words rang through my ears.

A bleed in the back of my head

and a tear in my neck, which was bleeding to.

I cried. I cried so hard.

Tears of sadness, tears of fear.

How could this be happening to me?

How do I cope now? How do I get my life back?

Will it be 'Goodbye?'

I HAD A STROKE

15th November 2022

It was the day my whole life changed yet again. It was never expected, but I guess I was not surprised after how I had been feeling for so many months. I was broken all over again. I was scared and felt so alone in yet another new world. My stroke was a bleed on the brain at the back of my head and a bleed in the back of my neck, caused by my arteries splitting open. Not something I ever expected to happen! The damage I was left with from my stroke was loss of sight, no use of left upper body, lack of balance and co-ordination leaning to one side, also affecting my short -term memory. I live in fear of having another stroke which is hard not to and all I want to do is cry and shout 'why me' as I fight to survive.

My stroke has taken away what life I had. The life I knew, in which I was trying to cope with. My depression and anxiety are at rock bottom, the worst they have ever been. Having the stroke has changed my everyday life including having difficulty finding the right words most of the time and understanding what others are saying. It has left me feeling irritable, forgetful, and totally confused, affecting my ability to control my mood and emotions, making me constantly snappy and taking even more to heart than I did before. My memory is rubbish and I have such a poor attention span now that it frustrates me so much. I have constant outbursts for no real reason.

It has changed my whole life, as if it wasn't hard enough before, but now I feel like I have lost it completely. It is not what it was and I know it is never going to be the same again, because, my limitations have changed and a lot of adaptions have had to be made for me to cope. I never believed my mental health and physical health could possibly get any worse than it already is! All because of this stroke.

It feels as though this is how my life is to be from now on.

WHY WOULD THEY NOT LISTEN?

It was the end of March.

I bashed the back of my head on the corner of the cupboard as it
swung back.

It did not bleed… but oh how dizzy I felt.

From that day things were never the same again

and this went on for months.

The continuous headaches in the back of my head,

My blood pressure through the roof.

Three trips to A and E.

But no one listened, no one did a thing.

They kept telling me they were migraines!!

Why wouldn't anyone listen?

Why was I the only one that knew something was wrong?

My blood pressure just kept on rising. Dangerously rising.

But no one looked at why?

I knew I was not right.

I knew something was wrong.

I was getting worse

But they just NEVER listened.

Why would they not listen?

IF ONLY THEY LISTENED

It was March 2022 when I bashed the back of my head as I bent down to pick up what I had dropped, the cupboard swung back. I had stood up and hit the back of my head on the corner of the cupboard. Wow!! How that hurt. I came over dizzy but ignored it and carried on with my life. Over the next few weeks, I began suffering with severe headaches in the back of my head. I began feeling extremely unwell and my blood pressure was extremely high. From then on, I turned to professional help but was ignored by the fact anything was wrong. No one listened. Three times I went to A and E and after being left for hours I was constantly told it was migraines. But I knew they were more than just migraines. I knew something was seriously wrong.

As months went on, it just got worse and worse until November 2022. I had a stroke. As you can imagine this absolutely broke me. Why did they not listen to me? Why didn't they believe me when I kept saying something was wrong? The fact that my blood pressure was dangerously high and just kept going up but instead I was just put on another blood pressure tablet. I will never forgive them, because they never listened. They are to blame. Because they never listened. I have been feeling so alone with this. Not being able to do anything by myself. I was left partially sighted and unable to drive for what has felt like a lifetime. My memory is appalling. I forget things all the time and I struggle to find the right words and understanding what others are saying most of the time. I am more tired than ever before and I feel so frustrated and angry all the time.

The ones I believed I could count on, the professionals, let me down. My symptoms were dismissed again and again, but I knew something was wrong. I knew my own body. I wish they had listened, then I would not have had my stroke. I would not have lost my sight. They refused to listen to what I was saying, instead shoved me on another blood pressure pill and told me I had migraines! What a joke.

If only they listened….

THE PERSON I KNEW

How am I to heal?

How am I to re- build my life?

My soul is damaged now

from all this pain and brokenness.

I get told to keep fighting but I feel so weak.

Who am I to believe that things will get better?

I weep, for I believe there is no hope

as I try so hard to live in this world that I know

is to be from now on.

I never asked to be dealt this 'stroke'

but it came and took hold of me.

Destroyed all that I had left of my already broken soul.

How do I survive?

Please....

Take my hand and show me the way.

Show me…

How do I re-live a life when I am so broken all over again.

When I feel I am never to get back to who I was.

The person only 'I knew.'

IT IS ALL NEW TO ME

When I had my stroke, it felt as though my whole life was caving in, the day it happened. I did not think for one minute that I was having a stroke. But, on this day, November 2022, something changed for the worse. I was attempting to hang some wet washing on my airer, only I was struggling to hang each item. I felt disorientated, then as I got up and tried to walk away, I was all over the place as if I was drunk! I was unable to walk straight, but I was also having trouble focusing. This scared me so much, that I sat and cried, then I rang emergency services still unaware of what was happening to me. Just a short time before, I could see, I could walk in a straight line. I had been aware of all that was going on.

Since my stroke, I have been affected in more ways than I thought I could ever be. Physically, psychologically, mentally, and emotionally. I feel like I have lost what little life I had. My moods and personality have changed so much. I get angry and frustrated at the slightest thing and upset so easily. My anxiety is the worst it has ever been and I constantly feel irritable, reacting to things that would not normally annoy me. I am having even more trouble sleeping than I have ever had. I have weaknesses in my arms and legs. I have had to learn how to scan with my eyes, as I was partially sighted after my stroke. Most of my sight has returned, only my peripheral vision is only 80% and unfortunately, that is how it will forever be now. I still have pain, numbness and tingling sensations throughout my arms, hands, legs, and feet. I am so forgetful all the time. Sometimes I say things yet do not even remember saying them. People tell me things and I fail to remember and sadly, that is how it is going to be, as that part of my brain is dead.

I understand my brain needs rest. It needs to re-wire itself, however, I do not need people shouting at me. I need people to be patient with me, to be more understanding. I know my stroke recovery is going to take time. It is hard to predict just how long, how soon, as frustrating as it is for me. But there is also so much that will never come back. I have to learn to live with the way I am.

But I always want others to remember ….

That this is all new to me…

MY DAD

My Dad…

His heart was always full of kindness,

carrying such warmth.

His smile always lit up a room

and his words, so gentle.

I hate that I never got to say goodbye

before he took his last breath

and I cannot tell him how many tears I have cried since.

But he will always be in my memory,

he will forever be in my heart.

I will always be proud to say he is 'my dad.'

The kindest man, I ever knew.

Time will never change anything,

for I will always miss him and forever love him.

He will always be 'my dad'

and one day…

heaven will bring us together again.

I WILL ALWAYS MISS YOU DAD

19ᵗʰ January 2023 R.I.P

I still can't believe he is gone. I still wake each day thinking it is not real and that if I was to ring him, I would hear his voice at the end of the line.

The day my dad passed away, I wished so much that he could have stayed. I will always wish he had more time. The day he passed away, I kept pretending that everything was alright, but it was not…It still isn't. My fake smile is hidden beneath the pain that I hold inside, when all I want to do is cry…so loud. The day he passed away was so suddenly that I never had the chance to say 'goodbye' and as the cries of my tears hang over me and the pain of the loss of him, the absence, breaks me into tiny pieces and drains my soul, my heart shatters until I have nothing left. I am so angry at myself, that I never got to see him as much as I should have. I miss him so much. I miss his voice. I miss not having him here and I wish so much, that I had told him more that I love him, instead of expecting him to know, to assume. I will never get over him passing even though I know he is with so many that will take care of him where he is now. I am lost that he is no longer here, as the sadness eats away at me making me realize how much I miss him. I cannot think of him as gone because it hurts too much, so I will keep him here in my heart, forever in my thoughts, knowing I will see him again one day. I will never say 'goodbye' but rather 'see you later.' I have so many memories. The tents he built out of his work planks, ladders, and dust sheets, when I was a kid. The walks we went on when he used to shout 'snake.' A joke of course, but I always believed there really was a snake. He taught me to ride my first bike even though I was so scared! Rushing me to hospital to have stitches when I cut my knee open. He held my hand as I cried. I wish he was here to hold my hand now, to wipe away my tears that I cry for him.

Be at rest now Dad. I will see you on the other side. But know, that I do love you very much and I hope that one day I will find the strength to be as strong as you and fight for my life, fight until the very end.

Just like you did….

I AM BROKEN

I hurt so much…

Because all the things that have happened to me

and in all the times I have kept them to myself,

instead of opening and pouring my heart out…

I am locked away inside my broken heart

and long to escape this burden of pain.

To chase away the dark thoughts that fill my head,

to step into a real world of normality.

But my soul is trapped on this slippery slope of tomorrow.

I am broken…

But nobody picks up my pieces and tries to help fix me.

Even when I am falling…

There is nobody around to catch me.

I know you cannot see it in my face

I know you cannot see it in my eyes

But can't you take the time to notice

That I am broken inside.

BROKEN

(Trigger Warning: This letter contains mention of rape/abuse)

From way back to now even, everything seems broken and I have this awful feeling inside, where everything is churning up and I want to scream out all that is eating away at my inner self. It is overwhelming and sometimes frightening because I do not know how to deal with it. Just as I think I have started to try and move forward; it suddenly shows up again and again and then I realize it is never going to go away. For such a long time, I have kept so many things well hidden, not told a soul about. I have felt so sad for such a long, long time. What with my mental health disorders and my physical health disorders, the violent rape of both physical and mental abuse that 'demon' has tortured me with. The adoption, the sad deaths of so many loved ones.

Then out of nowhere, my partner had a stroke. He passed away before I even had time to get my head around what was happening to him. Things were going so perfect between us until suddenly he was no longer here. It absolutely broke me. I never believed I could hurt so much. Then I had a sudden stroke myself, which knocked me back even more than I was already feeling. I believed I was going to die, after what happened to John. I did not think for one minute that I could ever recover. I was not strong enough for starters and here I was broken all over again. Then my dad suddenly passed away, the one man I always looked up to. The man that I was so proud to call 'my dad.'

I really believe, I am broken. The number of times I have fallen and made so many attempts to get back up. But, not anymore. I have hit rock bottom and I have come to realize, that there is no getting back up for me. My fragile body has finally splintered into smithereens and there is no going back. No picking up the pieces and gluing me back together.

I am no more.

TROUBLED MIND

I am sorry, but I am done.

I have cried so much, there are no tears left.

I have tried so hard, but I have no fight left inside of me.

I am tired of waiting for something that never comes.

Fighting my battles that you have no idea about.

Dragging me to the depths of hollowness,

tugging on my frail heart.

Do not tell me to be strong when my body is feeling so weak.

Or that you are here for me when I am all alone.

I am broken on the floor,

my heart shattered into tiny pieces,

crushed beneath the weakness of my bones,

as I hide behind my blackened eyes.

Please let my thoughts not be a cascade of nightmares anymore

Do not let my words fade into the distance.

Do not leave me to tangle up in my emotions.

Please do not let me drown in my troubled mind.

Help me

MY MIND IS TROUBLED

It is such an excruciating pain, to wake each morning in hope that things will be different, when in fact, they are the same as the day before, if not worse. The warming rays of the awakening sun, may be shimmering through the gaps in my blind and a cool breeze blowing through the slightly ajar window. But the way the light rests beneath my skin, does not change how I think and feel. I am tired of carrying this heavy weight of sadness and pain and fear. Trying to talk myself out of all that keeps pulling me down, but my voice continues to echo through empty walls as I lie staring into an empty space.

This is me- Like I am drowning. A massive weight is pulling me down under water. Some-how I keep going, but it is hard to keep on fighting these feeling of hopelessness and overwhelming sadness. I feel like there is no reason to carry on for everything feels pointless. My head full of negative thoughts, my life a failure. There is no calm both physically and mentally and however hard I try; nothing seems to clear my troubled mind. Every day and night I cry, because my tears tell me that my mind is battling every single thought and feeling, and I am trying to beat them and the demon that forever burdens my life, yet I never succeed. I never even have time to prepare myself for what is to come next. It just happens.

I just hope that no one gives up on me- Like I have given up on myself, for I can no longer fight these battles that forever strip me from the deep wounds I carry. My broken pieces, scattered in the darkness that live among the spaces in my world of 'fear.' I scream out several times, at the voice inside my head, as it keeps on reminding me repeatedly, of the person I am.

But no one hears me…..

I WONDER

(Trigger Warning: This poem contains mention of suicidal thoughts)

I wonder…

How many more times do I have to take the pills

to make you realize this is serious.

How many more times do I have to sit in a corner

sobbing my heart out, wishing I could be anywhere but here-

I wonder…

How many times do I have to tell you that I am so, so crushed.

How much longer do I have to live in this world

where I bury myself inside my broken shell.

I wonder…

How much longer do I have to go on pretending that I am okay

because you cannot see what is happening.

You cannot see the pain I feel deep within my withered soul

and when I am no longer here because you ignored me.

I wonder…

If you will cry for me then.

WILL ALWAYS WONDER

(Trigger Warning: This letter contains mention of suicidal thoughts)

I always thought that the one friend I believed I could turn to, would always be around when I really needed them. But how wrong was I! I know they have never really understood my mental health but neither have they ever taken the time to try and understand. So many times, I have needed them to be with me, yet so many times they have let me down. It is so, so hard and soul destroying the fact that I have mental health disorders and I kind of hope that the one that calls themself my friend, would be there for me like they always drum into my head that they would be, no matter what. Yet when the time comes and I am at the lowest of the lows and I can only hope that by reaching out to that friend, that they would help me. But instead, they let me down big time. When I am feeling so alone and frightened. Lost and confused. Like there is no way out! They have no idea what it is like to feel like this. When I tell them I need to talk to them because I do not trust myself in how I am feeling and that I am so desperate. They have no idea what it feels like to be like this? To feel so alone? I am suicidal and they refuse to help. I want to end my pain and I try so hard to talk to them, wanting them to be at my side, to listen to how desperate I am…All I want is for them to show that they care like they keep saying they do and yet they refuse to help, to listen. To even try and understand why I am feeling like I am. They don't even acknowledge the tears that I am crying because I am so scared of what I will do next. Yet they call themselves a friend?

All too often I have believed I can rely on my friend when I really need them, when in fact, this just proves a point that I cannot always count on them. I am not saying that all friends are like this but it is very important that I can tell someone that I can trust and that will listen. Yet this clearly is not that 'friend.' But if they needed me to be there for them, I would. I would be by their side and I would listen.

I wonder, if I was no longer here 'would they cry for me then?'

SOMEWHERE

I wish I was somewhere…

Somewhere out of where I am, a place far away.

Where there is no pain, no fear, no sadness

where children happily play.

Caressed by graceful cotton clouds and

warming rays of the awakening sun.

Where I can be free and happy,

all my pain and sadness can be undone.

I wish I was somewhere…

Another place but here.

A place filled with undulating beauty

that lays stretched from ear to ear.

I wish I was somewhere…

Out of my darkness and into the light.

Where trees bow with mellow grace and birds twitter in the night.

I wish I was somewhere…

To take away my pain.

I wish I was in Heaven

to feel free, once again.

ONE DAY... I WILL BE SOMEWHERE ELSE

My world has changed so much since my mental and physical health has kicked in and my loved ones have passed away and my stroke has taken what life I had. I wish so many times that I could be in heaven. Not just because I want to be there, but to escape from this sadness, pain, fear and struggles I am trying to cope with. The turmoil of my everyday life that I so long to leave behind. The darkness that smothers my every- day living. The pain that I long to break free from. I am tired of fighting. I am drained from the tears that I continually cry. Trying to hold on to life. Trying to hold on to hope. I am tired of breathing. I just want to be at peace. One day I will be somewhere else, far away, in heaven. I know that then, I can finally be at rest. No more suffering.

I believe heaven to be a place of beauty, of natural wonder surrounded by every coloured flower possible. The walls and paths of pure gold and waters clear as crystal. A place full of love and perfect peace. Where all my loved ones that have gone on before me shall be waiting to greet me. I believe that one day... I will be somewhere else. Somewhere so serene, so picturesque. I believe that God has a time and a plan laid out for my life, for all our lives.

I am not sure of those that are reading this will have the same beliefs as me, but I know it is the one thing that keeps me going. Knowing I will be going to a place of peace and tranquillity. A new world of love, happiness, and kindness.

362

There may be many of you reading this right now, who do not believe there is a heaven! In that case, I am truly sorry that you feel that way. Afterall, we cannot all be the same, can we? But I for one, am so glad that I believe there is. If I am honest, it is one of the thoughts that I have that really keeps me going, knowing that one day I will be going there, to be with my loved ones again, to see all those that have gone before me and know that all those that I leave behind, will someday join me once again. No more tears or pain, just perfect peace.

SUICIDE SURVIVOR

(Trigger warning: This poem contains mention of suicidal thoughts)

It was all just too much for me to go on living and oh,

how sorry I am that I could never tell you how my soul was so broken.

I could not live any longer in my world of pain with the suffering that I faced each day.

I believed I was a failure as I lived in this darkness, trying my best not to fall apart,

hoping that this would be the time I would not wake up.

There was no way out of this darkness and despair.

Only one way I could go, to end my forever pain.

I may have seemed unbreakable to you, but I wasn't, and I finally gave up…

My pills lined up…then one by one… I swallowed.

Taking the final one as tears ran down my cheeks.

You did not know what I was feeling! Or how much I was hurting!

So much so, that I could not possibly live anymore-

I chose to leave this world behind, to fade into the light, to take me to another world of peace.

Slowly, I drifted off to sleep, silently waiting…

Then a voice whispered in my ear 'YOU SURVIVED.'

The pain I had suffered for so long……

I now must live all over again.

DO I HAVE TO LIVE?

(Trigger warning: This letter contains mention of suicidal thoughts)

This was a poem I wrote shortly after one of my suicide attempts, from how I was feeling to just one of the times that I was so desperate that I could not go on living any longer. Instead of reaching out for help when I thought I was all alone I believed it was the right thing to do. Not for anyone else, but for me. I wanted to escape the feelings and end the unbearable thoughts that I was having. I had reached a point in my life where I felt suffocated, where I was so desperate. It seemed at the time to be the only answer, the only solution. It is probably one of the worst pains I have ever felt (along with when my loved ones have passed away). The pain of suffering, the pain of feeling as though my life has deteriorated to a point where I feel I have no choice. Telling someone that I want to die is one of the hardest things I have ever said, because so many people label it as 'attention seeking' or that 'I am being selfish' and that I should not do something so bad. But I don't want to be made to feel guilty. It is help and support that I need and until anyone has experienced the utter depths of despair, then those people should keep their opinions to themselves. So many times, I have not been able to see a way out for myself, because it feels as though I am continuously fighting my battles.

Noone would ever know if I was sat in the middle of the night penning the words together of my suicide note, whilst everyone is sleeping. How would anyone know? I am pretty sure many are thinking, how can I possibly take it upon myself to even want to end my life? What about all my loved ones? Yes of course, I think about them all. But imagine what kind of pain I am in to get to the point of wanting to end it all?

I have been in this place several times. I know what it is like to want to die. I know the feeling of hopelessness and to anyone that has ever been there, you know what it feels like to....

TIME

Time is…

An element that I cannot control.

A measure of life that has gone by

in seconds, minutes, hours, even years.

Time is…

A memory that has destroyed me,

that stalks my mind.

That I fear of never getting over

or ever moving on.

Time is…

Of being lost.

A traumatic feeling

never again to find one's way

Time is…

Moments that take away your life

Time is…

Then and now.

Time is…

Not my future.

WHAT IS TIME?

(Trigger Warning: This letter contains mention of the demon and dying)

For me, time is a continuous existence from past to present. The past…All that has happened to me. The present… All that is happening to me now. Time is not my future for I have lost my way. Time to me is an element that is not going to change. I guess with over 36 years of living in silence, it has made my time stand still as I have not been able to move on, and with so much disruption in my life, my daily clock is never set right either. It feels as though there is always so much pressure, because my life is constantly challenging. All I think about is the 'time' of the demon. My mind is preoccupied with the fear of him. He destroyed me and he is what has stopped me from living my life. 'Time' has stood still in that moment and I believe I will forever be in that moment, because he holds me hostage in all that he did. I will never be free as the thoughts and feelings of that time are still with me. It may be okay for people to say stop living in the past, that time has been and gone but believe me it is not as easy as that. When something so traumatic has happened, like it has to me, it is not by choice that I still cling on to what has happened, but there is no escaping from it which is why I have PTSD. I do not enjoy being like this. All the time in the world is never going to make any of this go away because this is my life. Time is not my future.

As the clock ticks away and I sit thinking about how I feel, physically and mentally and how much calmer and gentler my life could be if I did not have to live this way anymore. I sit, taking in the silence, thinking how it could be if I could escape my dark world of pain and trauma. The battles I face daily, of thoughts and feelings. As the clock ticks away, I count the seconds before I have to say the word 'sorry.' Sorry that I have to cut my life here, but I am living in sheer agony and it is destroying me. I am so fragile, that I cannot hold my frame together any longer. I am not strong enough. I have to die…

As the clock ticks away, I count the seconds down before I break free from my life in which I have suffered more than anyone will ever know.

Tick tock… Tick tock…Tick tock

I AM GONE

Drowning in myself…

From my brokenness that I hold within me.

As the cracks in my heart break into tiny pieces.

Numb from the pain coursing through my veins,

barely able to move, as the weight of the world

crushes down on my weary body.

Lost in this coldness that I live in…

Trying to survive in my world of darkness.

But it never gets any easier.

There will never be any light for me,

never will I find the path to hope,

to happiness.

Nor will I escape from the torture

that is etched in my brain.

I am falling…

I am giving up…

I am gone.

GIVING UP

(Trigger Warning: This letter contains mention of rape and suicidal thoughts)

Life presents me with such difficulties, making it very hard to overcome and every day becomes more and more of a struggle to survive. Sometimes life feels so painful for me that I have endless negative thoughts, until I reach a point that I want to give up on everything, and the only solution is to end my life. I have never wanted to hurt my loved ones, my family. I just want the pain to stop. I am tired of how my life is, how it is making me feel, which is why I have this urge so many times, to want to leave my life, because I feel so lonely, trying to get through each day, feeling the way I am. Noone sees just how much I need saving, as I fight my battles that not a soul knows about. I weep beneath the sky, waiting for the sun to shine down on me, to comfort me, only it never happens. So, instead, I dream under the blanket of stars, for my life to try and piece itseld back together, for I am tired of spiralling deeper and deeper into these whirlwinds of darkness. But where is the light? It still doesn't show itself in my world, which is why, when I say I am giving up, that I want to give up living. It is not just because I am done with all the fighting that I have had to live through all these years. Yes, I am tired of fighting, but most of all, I am done with the 'suffering.' I cannot live my life like this anymore. My head filled with torture and pain of all that I have been through and still going through. My body broken, my life in pieces. I am tired of carrying this torture that eats away at my bones daily. I want to shine again, but instead, I live in this dark world that even I don't recognize anymore! I feel suffocated now, trying so hard to survive each day, in hope it will get easier, but it doesn't. So, you see, it isnt about the fighting- I am suffering more than you realize and I can't do it anymore. I cannot pretend anymore. Much of my life, well, since I was abusively raped, I knew things were going to be different. I knew my world had changed. I never felt suicidal until the rape. From that night, I wished so much, that I would never wake up. What the 'Demon' did to me that night- He stole so much from me, including my identity. This is not the life I have wanted, yet here I am still walking this path I walk. Wishing so much that it could take me on a different route and take away what happened to me. But, it never does. It is not about just giving up. It is about getting away from what keeps hurting. Putting an end to it...

GOODBYE

(Trigger Warning: This poem contains mention of suicidal thoughts)

The heartache continues, my tears they still fall,

for the hurt is still with me, I cannot face it at all.

People try to talk to me, but I am not there,

for my heart is full of sadness, it is unfair.

I cannot help but get so low and so down,

guess no one would miss me if I was no longer around.

I often get this feeling I could just fade away,

leave this world behind me, never to face another day.

No place is left for me no more, no longer do I belong,

love is no more all is still, for me, my life has gone.

So, if I leave this life behind me, say goodbye to all the pain,

I can close my eyes forever, not a tear will shed again.

But one last thing I must ask, before I say goodbye,

no spoken words just a gentle hug

and hold me as I die.

HOLD ME AS I DIE

(Trigger Warning: This poem contains mention of suicidal thoughts)

Yes, this is a dark and very unsettling poem that I have written. I wrote this a while ago, just before attempting to take my own life. One of many…

This is me, being open to something that I have faced several times in my life and all too often, being in the darkest of places ever where I have been at the lowest of my lows. This is about the thoughts and feelings I have going on in my life and I am sure there are many others like me but I have not written this for people to just think 'Oh my word' this is strong stuff … But to let people know that this does happen and I apologize if this upsets anyone, it really is not my intentions, but I need to get this out there.

Suicide feelings are the worst feelings ever and the worst part is the pain, because it is the most unbearable pain that you can just never imagine ever ending. You feel so desperate that you believe it is your only choice. You feel so alone and lost. Frightened and confused. No-one but yourself can ever imagine how you are feeling, because unless they have gone through the same thing themselves, it cannot be compared. I know there are going to be a lot of people that know me who will be reading this, especially members of my family. I know my mum especially and my sisters and my sons are going to be so hurt to know that I have been in this dark life and that they had no idea, because I know they would have supported me. But how could I tell them?

How could I say that I want to die? How would anyone understand if I said I want to end my life? That I feel as though I have no life here anymore! I just want to close my eyes and drift away. If I must be alone when I go, then so be it. I always thought it would be right to die alone but if I can have all my loved ones around me, then I would love them all to be at my side. To be with me until I take my last breath. Have one last hug and hold me as I die.

AS I DIE ALONE

(Trigger Warning: This poem contains mention of suicidal thoughts)

I lied and said I was busy,

when really, I was sat alone with the silence that surrounded me.

As tears rolled down my sullen cheeks,

I buried myself under the blanket that covered my weary body.

Moments held in memory,

like petals of rosebuds in my hands,

holding on to life, holding on to hope.

The light dimmed as sadness took away my smile.

I knew I was not enough. I would never be enough.

Memories filled my head,

as my eyes closed to my softened cries.

Fear tortured my mind as loneliness drained my soul,

and grief broke my heart.

Left hanging from this thread of life

in this barren room of eternal darkness

dragging me to the depths of hollowness

as I die alone.

UNTIL I DIE

(Trigger Warning: This poem contains mention of suicidal thoughts)

The times I have said to people that I am busy…When honestly, I am sat alone sobbing my heart out wishing so much that I was not here anymore. If I could just end it all then it would stop all my pain. Oh, how easy it would be to just close my eyes and drift away into another world where there was no longer all this suffering I live with each day, alone. Grieving for my love I have lost. Grieving for the loss of my dad. Living in fear of something so bad occurring again, still re living what has happened to me over the years. My physical health and untold operations I have had to go through. My mental health that has deteriorated even more so since my stroke. My life at a stand-still as I re-live all the torture, the drowning of the life I cannot forget. Again and again, I have wanted to die. So many moments I have imagined my body to just fade away and die alone.

This makes me cry even though it is about me. This makes me cry because it is all so true.

How many times I have made out I am busy when in fact I have been sat alone crying my heart out, just wanting to be free from the pain that eats away at my fragile body. How many times I have just wanted to close my eyes and then when they open once more, I find I am in a better place. How many times have I overdosed but always come out the other side, when really, I have wished so much that I had died. So many times, I have said I have too much to do, when really, I have been sat at home planning how to end my life. It is not very often I plan it. Most of the times I just do it with no thought at all. Just wanting to end my sad, crippling, torturing, lonely life.

Noone understands what it feels like to be hanging by a thread. Living a life of fear. Waiting for some light to appear, but it never comes. No one will ever understand what it is like to be me. Only I know…. Only I can feel the pain amongst the 'silence' that surrounds me. My time will come…

Say your goodbyes as I die….

I WANT TO BE REMEMBERED

When my time comes and I take my last breath

I want to be remembered as the 'one'

that gave it her best shot.

That no matter what I had thrown at me,

I gave it my all-

Even with all the pain and heartache,

loss and loneliness, sadness, and fear-

I kept on going. I kept on fighting.

Even on the hardest days

I still made it through.

Even when I was convinced

I was falling, I clung on

to the fragile threads of my life.

When my time comes

and I take my last breath,

I just want to be remembered….

As the 'one' that never gave up.

REMEMBER ME

When my time is over, I want to be remembered in every best possible way. For my kindness, for my caring ways. For my smiles. For all the good I did in other's lives. For all the good times and the memories. I also want to be remembered as the one that 'never gave up.' No matter what was thrown at me in my lifetime, I kept on going. I want to be remembered as a kind and loving person to others, even though I was not to myself. It is true and I must accept that I cannot change who I became to myself, but rather be grateful that I always treated others with love, care, and respect. I want to be remembered as the 'imprint' in people's lives, heart, and mind as a funny, kind and understanding person. I may have been a 'failure' in my own life, but I hope I am remembered as a 'positive' person in all the lives that I touched and somehow made someone's day a little better. Remember me… When I am gone. When the seconds turn into minutes and minutes into hours. Then the hours turn into days and the days into weeks and so on. Remember me. I am sorry I had to leave, but I kept on going for as long as I possibly could. I never gave up. I fought until the end, with everything that was thrown at me.

When you are feeling lost or sad, look up to the sky and talk to me, I will hear you. We will always be connected. Speak about me to everyone you know and remember I will always be your guide.

Remember me as someone that although held on to so much for so many years, I eventually opened up about my life. Whatever my faults, whatever I have been through. I hope to be remembered for the one that kept on fighting, that kept on going.

For the one that never gave up.

WHEN I DIE

(TRIGGER WARNING: This poem contains mention of suicidal thoughts)

When I die-

Scatter my ashes in the beautiful serene garden of remembrance of
beauty.

Where butterflies fly in the wind and robins keep watch

on the branch of the blossom trees and flowers bloom

in the summer breeze.

Where pathways wind through untold tales of the forest of purity

and silence lies among the trees that stand in the woodland of love.

When I die-

Do not think of me as gone, for I will be by your side always.

I will be the love that surrounds you,

the butterfly that dances in the scented air.

The leaves that flutter carelessly in the autumn wind.

Your guiding light that rests beneath your skin.

I will be with you in your every step- in life

and give you the strength you need to get you through each day.

I will comfort your soul with peace and protect you

throughout your journey,

as you hold on to all the memories that we made.

HOLD ON TO THE MEMORIES

(Trigger warning: This letter contains mention of dying)

When I die, I will no longer live in this world of fear, pain, sadness, and bad memories. I believe that when I leave here, I will no longer live a tortured day and night. When my time comes, I will no longer have to suffer. I will be away from here. But I do not want you to be sad, but to know that I am free. Free from the pain that I was carrying. I do not want you to think of me as gone.... For I will be all around. In the butterflies that fly free in the wind. In the birds that sing their merry tunes. In the trees that blow softly in the gentle breeze. I will be in all that surrounds you- In every step you take and guide you throughout your journey, as you hold on to all the memories that we made.

I want to be remembered as the one that always gave generously and I do not just mean giving my last penny, but always loving, always kind and always respectful. I want to be remembered for always having time for others too, for helping, to lending a hand whenever I could no matter how low I felt or how much pain I was in. I kept it hidden. But I still found the strength to carry on. I want to always be remembered for respecting all those around me. For always treating everyone the same way that I have always wanted to be treated. I always want to be remembered as the one that loved. The one that gave so much.

But most of all…

I want to be remembered for all the memories that we made and for you to keep them in your heart and to always remember me.

'It is all any of us ever want when we die'…

TAKE ME TO THE OTHER SIDE

Take me to the other side…

Where I can feel at peace

Where everyone can understand me

and where calmness is released.

Take me to the other side…

Where I no longer must explain,

how I am feeling and why I am so broken.

No longer will I be in pain.

Take me to the other side…

Where I no longer must struggle to

keep myself whole.

Instead, my arms shall spread like new born petals

as they calm my restless soul.

Take me to the other side…

where I can finally be at rest.

With my loved ones again, to make new memories

and my heart is once again blessed.

TO THE OTHER SIDE

I have wished for this so many times. A huge part of me has wanted to be on the other side. For my hand to be taken and to be led the way to a beautiful new world. To be free from my feeling of brokenness. To leave this suffocating world behind.

To finally be at peace...

To finally be free...

To finally be at rest...

I once had a near death experience. Whilst undergoing an operation, I remember a bright light appearing in which I began to walk towards. As I looked back, all my family were stood in a line, crying, begging for me to stay. I felt so sad at the thought of leaving them, yet so calm and relaxed and intrigued as to what I was about to see on the other side. I was not scared at all, but by the time I went to walk further, the light disappeared and I woke up!

Who would not want to be in a forever place with complete happiness, to no longer suffer. No more sadness or pain. No more crying. No more pretending. No more darkness. Just purity and light. To be with loved ones again. How beautiful would this be?

There are so many things I can only imagine, after all I do not know exactly what I will see until I get there. But I believe that one day, I will be in a place where I belong. A place on 'the other side.'

God is the one I must keep on believing in and everything else will come to me.

HEAVENS' GATE

The day will come when I will meet my loved ones

Where the moon and the stars shine like they have never shone before.

To the place where I can be by their sides, together, once more.

Where the open space is filled with the air

that we all once again breathe.

A place of peace and healing together,

where we never have to leave.

The undulating beauty that lies before our eyes,

as flowers line our path

and cotton wool clouds fill the skies.

They may be gone from my life, but will forever

be here in my heart.

For one day, we will be together,

never again to be apart.

But until that moment comes

I must simply wait…

Wait for the day that they call me home…

Where we will meet 'At Heavens gate'

HOME IN HEAVEN

My time will come....

When I leave this world behind to join my loved ones in beautiful Heaven. A place of peace for me, for us all. I long for the day that my loved ones will meet me at heaven's gate and knowing I will see all those that have gone before me and all that shall follow me is the love that I hold in my heart. No more suffering and never to be apart again. My time will come... When I will be free from all this pain that I hold inside my fragile body. To be set free into a beautiful new world.

If like me, you have your beliefs in the afterlife, how amazing is it to believe that we will be with our loved ones that have gone on before us, but also those that will follow us later. Total peace. Serene and Calm. Fresh air, freedom and no more pain or sadness. Just beautiful.

I can only imagine... Dazzling shades of colour, stretching as far as the eye can see with pathways of gold laying stretched in front of me, as red, white, and yellow roses shower their petals on the ground where I walk. The sound of organs playing and voices of angels singing in the most beautiful harmonies. Heaven in my eyes, will be a symphony of music filled with perfectly pitched voices. Everyone wearing white linen, pure as the snow and fitted perfectly to every individual person. All around will be so clean, a world that could never be imagined as so beautiful. The scenery as striking as paradise and the scent of fresh flowers bursting throughout the air...

I do not know what exactly I will find when I reach the other side but my vision is my vision and when your time comes, you are more than welcome to join me there…

I CRY

I cry... For all the years I have had to cope by myself with my mental health and physical health disorders because I could not admit anything was wrong. For all the depression, panic and anxiety, loneliness, darkness, and fear. Feeling broken and trying so hard to survive. Thinking there was no place here for me. For every bit of pain that I have tried so hard to deal with alone because I was too ashamed to ask for any help. But I am gradually being more open and starting to be listened to.

I cry...For the sadness I carry, for all the times I miss my loved ones, unable to bring them back. For the time I will never get back with them, instead spend my life waiting until I meet them on the other side. For all the moments I have sat alone with my grief, trying so hard to survive in this troubled mind of mine keeping it hidden and dealing with it by myself. But I could not do it and now I have finally asked for help.

I cry …For the stroke I had that took away what life I was trying so hard to live. That took away my sight, the strength and usage of my left hand, my memory. Unable to read or write, unable to drive. Trying so hard to deal with what ability it has left me with. But here I am, on a slow road to recovery, attempting to achieve a life. A life in which I never believed I would get a second chance at.

I cry …For all the times I have attempted to take my own life, to escape from this pain that has been clouding over my body for so long. For all the moments I have sat alone unable to see a way forward, desperately wanting to give up. But now I finally have professionals that listen to me and understand me. All I can hope for, is that in time I will be able to slowly move forward.

I cry …For all that I have been through over 36 years and have held onto all this time, not telling a soul. Keeping silent because I was too scared. Yet here I am writing this book telling not just my family, but all those that read this. Sharing with you all, my deepest secret.…

CRYING

My reason for writing this poem is because with all that I have been through and still going through. For all my mental health Disorders. My PTSD, my depression and anxiety. For all my physical health and every bit of pain I have had to live with and still living with, including my stroke. For my grief after losing my love, my dad and all my other loved ones and for all my tears I have cried and continue to cry. For all the sad moments that I have attempted to take my own life, to try to escape from my fears, my sadness, my pain. For all that I have lived with for over 36 years including the traumatic rape that I have kept silent until now. The baby I had no choice but to give up. The constant flashbacks that have broken me, that destroy my life each and every day and night.

For now, I may keep struggling and I may mess up, I may make mistakes along the way. I may have many a breakdown of tears and screams and I may have days of weakness and hopelessness, but I pray that I will try so hard to have much better days ahead. Days when I can start believing in myself for the first time ever! Life has been hard for me; this book says it all. But I have come this far, so I should keep fighting, shouldn't I?

Wherever I am at in life, only I can change it. I know I have always believed that things will never be any different, but I know now, that no one is going to change them for me. I may forever feel broken and always live in fear, but I have to keep holding on. I have to make some new choices, don't I? Choose to be free from all that keeps pulling me down, then, and only then, I might start to wander in the right direction in life. Start a new journey. Leave it all in the past and look to the future.

When I read back some of the poems in this book, I cannot quite believe that I am sharing these with the world! As hard as it has been, in a strange way, they have saved me. Because I do not have to hide anymore. You know my life. You know my deepest secret….

I cry…

Because, I did not realize just how 'brave' I was to finally be open and share my life with the world…

Until now.

AUTHORS AFTERWORD

Well, you have come to the end of no doubt one of the deepest books you may have ever read in your life and I sincerely apologize if by now you are sitting in tears. I can assure you I still cry when I read it. However, it is not my intention to make you cry, neither have I written this book to have people feel sorry for me. I have had to tell my story. I have had to write it for the world to see. I know some may never understand why I have told it and some will disapprove of the details that I share. But I am hoping that many of you will understand why I had to and many of you may just be thinking 'that's me' and never again will you feel you have to keep quiet…Never again will you have to feel ashamed …Never again will you have to feel alone…

I have written this book because I wanted you as the reader to try and understand that these things really do happen in life. Some of you may have read some of these poems and letters and thought just how much they may sound like yourself or even somebody you know and I want you to know that it is okay and that you do not have to hide them or keep them from people as I have learnt myself from the last 36 years and this is why I am like I am, because I never stepped forward, I never asked for help. I never admitted I had a problem, or an illness. Neither did I ever tell anyone about the brutal abuse I went through or the severeness of my attack. It took me until 2017 to first admit that something was wrong after several attempts to end my life. It was then that I realized just how much I needed professional help. I was referred to the acute mental health team in September 2018 where I was diagnosed with PTSD, severe depression and severe anxiety and allocated a mental health worker in December 2018 but then the covid came and I was not allowed to see her face to face which was so hard, as I felt alone. Phone calls are not the same when you are feeling at your lowest. Attempting to deal with everything that was going on in my life as well as all that had happened over the 36 years of my life. Sadly, my care co-ordinator had to leave and I felt totally alone again, not being able to see anyone face to face. I had to wait to be allocated another mental health worker, so you can imagine, I was right back to the beginning again. I was really struggling and then in 2020 my partner sadly passed away very suddenly and I sunk further and further. This was when I then attempted to take my own life again.

I was then allocated a new mental health worker and she was brilliant, to getting me as much help as possible, not just with her but with other organizations too, but unfortunately, she then left and I have since been allocated someone else. I have also been allocated a peer support worker and she has been a godsend for me. Also, a psychiatrist, that helps me with my meds. I have also been seen by a psychologist with regards to coping strategies and have since gone on to see a trauma psychologist.

I go to a group once a week run by Solent mind which has really been helping as it feels so good to be able to be open about everything. I really am hoping that with the right support I will be able to cope better with my life. It has been hard for me, because I have never been one to admit I need help or that something was seriously wrong with me probably because I spent most of my life from my 20's onwards putting on a front. Smile and pretend I was okay. But believe me, it really does catch up with you. I have had some professional help also from grief counsellor, stroke team and the neurology and sensory team too. I know there is nothing I can do about my physical health, that is something I have to live with.

My journey has been a long, painful road, but I am hoping that with all the right help I am now starting to get and all that is to come, that things can get better for me. I know that all these things that have happened to me will never disappear. Mentally, they will always be in my head and physically I will always suffer, but maybe I will learn how to cope better. I can only hope. If you or anyone you know are struggling then please contact the relevant number in which I have supplied at the end of this book. Please do not cope alone. Ask for help. Talk to a friend or a family member if you can. If you feel that you cannot, then please ring the necessary experts and ask for help.

I would like to say a huge thank you to all those that have joined me in reading my book and I hope that in time, each one of you, including myself, can break free from all the trauma of darkness that lives within us and come out the other side.

Much love Louise xx

MEET THE AUTHOR (And what is next)

Louise is an English writer, author, poet. Whilst she was born in Swindon, Wiltshire, she was raised in Woking, Surrey until she moved to Southampton, Hampshire in 1994. She is a mum to two sons and nan to six grandchildren. She has always loved writing and many moons ago she entered two poetry competitions in which she was very fortunate to have both published. 'To love in life…to love in Heaven' was published in an Anthology in 1996 and 'Baby Mine' was published in a book called 'The Hidden Grief' in 1998. Due to her physical health deteriorating and her mental health disorders being diagnosed, her writing was put on the back burner as they say.

If she had not already been through enough in her lifetime, sadly, in 2020, her partner John passed away very suddenly which absolutely broke her. It was then that she turned back to her writing again and wrote 'A Pocket Full of Love' (I wrote this for you) A collection of touching pieces of poetry capturing all the love, life, heartache, and loss in her lifetime with John. One of her greatest and proudest achievements ever. But also, one of the most emotional things to because it was written in memory of him, which will always be treasured. Louise writes to express her thoughts and feelings, for it is the only therapy that helps her to keep surviving. Her writing gives her the opportunity to tell of her pain and to let her emotions out. Writing for Louise is her way of letting out her true feelings.

Louise has several more books in the pipeline, in which she hopes to complete. One being a real tear jerker novel inspired by a true story of real events of love, life, and loss. She is also looking at writing another collection of poems and letters, a follow-on book from 'Broken.' Each piece will tell a story of where she hopes to be and how she hopes to cope better from the life in which she has struggled with.

Not to forget, but to hopefully move forward. To survive…. To live...

ACKNOWLEDGEMENTS

There are so many people I would like to thank having being so grateful to everyone's support and encouragement.

To my beautiful Mum for her endless support. Always listening, even when I have had moments of breaking down (which is very often). Always understanding me and trying so hard to keep me positive. For always being the person, I can turn to when my days are dark. None of this would have been possible without her, for she has stood by me during all my struggles. Supporting my whole writing journey and always having faith in me. Thank you will never be enough for everything she has done for me and still does for me.

To my lovely step-dad who always listens. Always sharing his caring words of positiveness, even through all my downs and negativity, he always knows the right things to say to try and keep my head held up high.

To my wonderful Dad, God rest his soul who was still here when I started writing this book but sadly passed away 19th January 2023. A huge thank you to him for being my dad. For being in my life and giving me so many wonderful memories that I will never forget.

To my amazing step-mum who is always at the end of the phone, to listen and to boost me up. To make me smile and laugh when I am not really feeling it. For being the strongest woman, I know.

To my beautiful sisters for all their support and smiles along the way. Although writing may not be their thing, they always support me with mine and I am so grateful for that.

To my brother in laws for caring. Although may not understand what I am about a lot of the time lol, but have a pretty good idea.

To my two amazing sons who have been my absolute reason for living which is why I am still here. For their support and kindness. For making me laugh at times when all I want to do is cry. For always having my back. For being the two most amazing men ever, making me so proud for who they are and for having them as my sons. For putting up with me when I have asked them about things that may not necessarily interest them, especially when I ask what they think of my latest book cover I have designed, just to change it again … and again … and again. Sorry!!

My wonderful daughter -in-law that has sat so many times listening to my down moments and understands my thinking. We are more alike than we like to admit!

To my six grandchildren from the smallest to the biggest, but always so very precious to me. They are all so very different in their own way, but all so very special.

To my amazing father-in-law who has been my absolute rock since John passed away. Keeping me going, always trying to make me smile and laugh and for supporting me every step of the way.

To my long-time amazing friend Mags, that has been my absolute rock through everything I have been through even when she has had tough times herself. Always been the friend that has been there for me when all the others have walked away.

To Peter Davey who has kept me strong whilst writing this book, even when I have felt lost and alone. His support has shone through like a beacon of light and guided me along the way. A huge thank you to him for continuing to believe in me the whole way through, even when I have not believed in myself. For putting a smile on my face when I have wanted so much to cry. I would never have achieved finishing this without his amazing support and without him, I would never have believed that there is hope for my future.

I would also like to thank the 'Write that book' group and 'How to be brilliant' group:

Michael Heppell for running such an amazing group, but mostly for giving me the confidence and encouragement to write my book or should I say 'books'(boooooks). Becoming an author would not have been possible without the support from him and I want to thank him immensely for helping me into believing in myself for the first time ever.

Derek Crysell   a special thank you to him for helping me with the publishing side of things with my first book. For his kindness and caring nature and for always making me smile with his funny jokes.

Sarah McGeough for all her support and kindness not just through my writing but also with my mental health. For her advice and for listening.

Lorraine Buxton for all her kindness and positivity that has kept me going, especially after my stroke.

Debbie Buxton for thinking of me every day and her kind messages that have kept me boosted. Not forgetting the amazing review, she gave on my first book. For all her support.

Alexis Scott A huge thankyou to her for her kind personal messages. For understanding me with my grieving and my struggles and my mental health. For simply 'getting' me especially when I have felt unimportant.

Belinda Rose Bond, **Debra Gledhill**, **Beth Jordan**, **Sue Trusler**, **RKJ Adams**, **Sally Sindall**, **Tanith Knox**, **Denise Montagnolo, and Coral Smith** for all their support and kind wishes and for always keeping me in their thoughts.

To all the amazing friends I have made in the group. There are far too many of them to thank individually for keeping me going and what a pleasure it has been to get to know them all. Their kindness and support has touched my heart in so many ways that I cannot thank them enough.

SUPPORT SERVICES

Please find attached some support services to anyone that may need any help or advice. I have provided some numbers that you may wish to use.

Samaritans UK

www.samaritans.org.uk

Call: 116 123

Shout

www.giveusashout.org

text :85258 to contact the shout team or text "YM" if you are under 19

Rape Crisis Centre UK

info@supportline.org.uk

Call: 01708 765200

Victim Support (24/7 support)

Victim support operates a 24/7 support line and live chat

service, every day of the year, offering specialist emotional and practical

support to anyone who has been a victim or a witness. You do not have to

have reported a crime to get help from Victim Support.

www. victimsupport.org.uk

Call: 0808 16 89 111

Stroke Support

helpline@stroke.org.uk

Call: 0303 3033 100

To talk to someone who understands what a stroke means.

Can provide information on support available. They offer

Stroke survivors a 30-minute call with a fully trained volunteer.

Cruse Bereavement Support

Cruse.org.uk

Call: 0808 808 1677

Printed in Great Britain
by Amazon

41472519R00238